C000061654

MINI

OWNER'S SURVIVAL MANUAL

K765 GCJ

In association with

MINI OWNER'S SURVIVAL MANUAL

JIM TYLER

ACKNOWLEDGEMENTS

First and foremost: Em, Dave and Chalkie for an education in car maintenance, repair and restoration. Friends and family for their encouragement. Neighbours for their tolerance, good humour and occasional (unsolicited) pearls of wisdom. Autodata for permission to use diagrams. Osprey for publishing the book and *MiniWorld* for supporting it. Canon, Yashica and Zenith for making cameras tough enough to withstand life in my workshop. And that's about it.

First published in Great Britain in 1996
by Osprey, an imprint of Reed Consumer Books Limited,
Michelin House, 81 Fulham Road, London SW3 6RB
and Auckland, Melbourne, Singapore and Toronto.

ISBN 1 85532 610 8

Editor • Shaun Barrington
Art Editor • Mike Moule
Designer • Leigh Jones

Printed in Hong Kong

Anyone who has owned a Mini will invariably have a tale to tell about repairing it. Despite its revolutionary, yet simple, design, the Mini seems more prone than most to breaking down, often at the most unfortunate moments. The Mini's incredibly compact powertrain makes working under the bonnet a bit tricky at times and unless you know the tricks of the trade, hours can be spent stripping threads and skinning knuckles to complete a 'five-minute' job.
The key to keeping your Mini on the road is a combination of good advice and regular maintenance – finding trouble spots before they develop into breakdowns is all important in the battle against wear and tear.
With so many Minis still on the road, a huge industry has grown up to cater for the modifiers, restorers and those just keen on keeping their cars running. Availability of spares is rarely a problem, although educated advice as to how to fit them and prevent further trouble is less easy to find. The *Mini Owner's Survival Manual* is the ideal book for everyone who cares for a Mini. It covers everything from the most basic repairs and maintenance to renovation of complex assemblies like the brakes and suspension. Jim Tyler – a Mini enthusiast himself – has written a book accessible to all types of enth[illegible]ast from the first-time owner to the more seasoned [illegible]hanic.
Of course for all the up to date news an[illegible] [illegible]ice on caring for your Mini, pick up a copy of *MiniWorld* every month from your newsagents, or take advantage of our subscription hotline number at the back of this book to have *MiniWorld* delivered straight to your door every month. Happy spannering!

Mike Askew
Editor – *MiniWorld*

For a catalogue of all books published by Osprey Automotive please write to:

The Marketing Department, Reed Consumer Books, 1st Floor, Michelin House, 81 Fulham Road, London SW3 6RB

Contents

Introduction

Sir Alec Issigonis was arguably the most inspired and inspiring automotive designer of all time. Few car designers aspire to such an innovative masterpiece as the Morris Minor, and most would be pleased to have such a car accredited to them: such a magnificent achievement would, of course, be recognised as the pinnacle of their career. But Issigonis went one better. Issigonis designed the Mini.

The Mini may have started life as a utilitarian runabout, a shopping car, but during its early years it endeared itself to all men for all kinds of reasons. The Mini was an essential fashion accessory for some in the 1960s, a world-beating rally car to others and a reliable, affordable, practical yet 'fun' car to the majority. Most importantly, the Mini was the car in which the post-war generation learned to drive, its first car, its favourite car.

And here we are, 36 years after the Mini's launch, still able to buy a brand new Mini from the original manufacturer. The reasons for the Mini's longevity? Firstly, the Mini was 'right' at the time of its launch and new variants have all filled the niche created and monopolised by the little car to date. Not so obviously, the Mini shared components with other vehicles from BMC/British Leyland; had it been launched with the proposed twin cylinder engine instead of the evergreen A series unit, then the Mini would quite possibly no longer be with us.

During the Mini's lifetime, other cars have come and gone, each generation more complex than its predecessor. The justification for growing sophistication is that it makes cars more reliable, sometimes more economical but, as a sophisticated car ages, it eventually deteriorates to the point at which many of its extra components begin to fail, one by one. What starts as a trickle of component breakdowns snowballs until the car becomes so expensive to keep on the road and so unreliable that the only economically viable course of action for the owner is to give up and scrap it. Not so for the uncomplicated Mini.

Not only does an ageing Mini possess fewer components to break down than many of its contemporaries, but those components are more readily available, generally cost rather less and are - though there are exceptions - usually a darn sight easier to replace. Maintenance and most repair work on a Mini is well within the capabilities of the DIY mechanic. If you choose to have servicing and repair work carried out professionally on an old Mini, you don't have to go to a specialised company because there can be few mechanics who are not thoroughly familiar with the Mini. But most Mini maintenance and repair work is well within the capabilities of any able-bodied owner.

Of course, the electronic ignition and fuel injection systems of the most recent Minis do make the cars less user-repairable but, unlike other modern cars, the current Mini does not have built-in obsolescence; when most cars are superseded, the spares availability slowly dries up, but there is already a huge industry dedicated to keeping Minis - recent and ancient - on the roads. Apart from fuel injection and ignition matters, I see no reason why the average DIY mechanic should not be maintaining his or her Mini for many years to come.

Thirty-five years separate old Mini No.1 and this Mini 35 Special Edition and, although the modern version is faster, plusher and generally does everything better than its forebear, both offer the driver exactly the same unique Mini experience.

621 AOK
L621 AOK

And that is what this book is all about. Buying and maintaining your Mini, with a look at the perils and pitfalls of restoration, and a guide to avoiding where possible - and dealing with where unavoidable - breakdowns. But first a brief look at the remarkable history of the Mini, and how to avail yourself of this wondrous little car (and a word to the wise regarding 'performance' and the driving experience).

Jim Tyler

The engine bay of the 1.3 injected Cooper is more crammed full than a tin of sardines - which makes working on the car rather more difficult than on early Minis.

THE 'COOKING' MINI

Owners of standard Minis who follow the motoring press might become dispirited when they find that most articles concern only custom or hotted-up Minis; and wonder whether, in driving their cooking Mini, they are missing out on something. They shouldn't.

I passed my driving test in a Mini and have owned a fair number since. Notably, there was the white honeymoon 850; before that came the 1966 Wolseley Hornet in which we somehow found room for self and intended plus a full drum kit (with 22-inch base drum), haring around the Midlands to gigs.

All of my Minis have been standard. None was noted for causing tail-backs. Then, as now, I hated being stuck behind slower drivers in vastly more powerful cars.

The standard Mini was never terribly good at overtaking, especially when trying to pass those drivers who raced between bends, (when the Mini behind was winding up to a respectable speed and gaining ground), but who cornered with brake lights ablaze, obliging the anguished Mini driver to follow them lamely and then watch them disappear towards the next bend, ready to repeat the sequence.

This led me to drop back so that I could coax the Mini up to an overtaking speed, calculated carefully so that when the corner-crawler exited a bend I'd be in the perfect position for overtaking and travelling fast enough to get past – given a clear road!

So what is the point of this potted history of (fairly dubious) roadcraft procedure? The point is that with the benefit of hindsight, I now realise that the low engine power of my Minis actually brought an unexpected bonus: in that driving the cars was much more *involving* than driving a more powerful car The more powerful and capable a car, the less effort it is to drive, the less rewarding it is to drive.

In any case, owning a Mni is not just about getting from A to B in the shortest possible time: it's about having fun along the way, or can be, with the right frame of mind. The fun comes in equal measure from the cooking and breathed-on varieties.

So, all you owners of standard Minis, admire the hotted-up steeds in the motoring press, secure in the knowledge that your own car is in no way inferior. There is no rule that says a boosted or customised Mini confers greater driving pleasure than the standard issue.

"Are you also a stylist?" **Battista (Pinin) Farina**
"No! I am an engineer." **Alec Issigonis**

"The most pleasing thing that has happened to me was my appointment to the Royal Society. I think I felt that too many fellows were academic and that an old ironmonger like me would help to redress the balance." **Sir Alec Issigonis**

(Quoted in *Mini – 35 Years On*, Rob Golding, Osprey, new ed. 1994; still the definitive Mini book.)

Stop Press: As this book is approaching the printer, Rover has announced that a successor to the Mini has been given the go-ahead; on sale perhaps as early as 1998. There has been speculation that 'Mini' may become a marque rather than a single car for the Rover/BMW group. It is not difficult today to design a better car 'on paper', but they surely know that to win the hearts of Mini fans everywhere, the *spirit* of Mini must be preserved!
More than ever, all Mini owners are custodians of a slice of British motoring heritage.

Chapter One

MINI – Legendary Survivor

Relatively few cars have a production run lasting more than five years, and fewer still make it past ten years. However good the cars – and modern cars are uniformly, boringly, 'good' – the majority lack any hint of special character to raise them above their contemporaries and ensure their production survival. A few radical designs prove so competent that, on cessation of manufacture by their original company, their tooling is sold to less well-off countries where manufacture continues, such as the evergreen VW Beetle in South America. Only one car design has proven so revolutionary yet unarguably 'right' in every respect that in the 1990s it is still being made by its original manufacturer in its country of origin over thirty-five years after its launch – and that car is the Mini.

Few cars enjoy even a ten year production life and many don't last five. The Mini has not only been in production during five decades, it is still being manufactured by its original maker – albeit under different ownership.

In the late '40s and early 1950s, the roads of the UK were populated in the main by old-fashioned, over-weight and consequently fuel-guzzling saloons, and amongst general post-war shortages there was an on-going petrol shortage. There was an obvious need for less thirsty cars, and most UK manufacturers started development programs to this end. The Morris Motor Company was fortunate to have a brilliant young design engineer, Alec Issigonis, who designed a prototype small saloon car

Issigonis' first masterpiece – the Morris Minor. In addition to sharing its designer with the Mini, the Minor also set new standards in roadholding and handling, just as the Mini did in 1959.

dubbed the 'Mosquito' which entered production in 1948 as the Morris Minor. At the time, no other car handled quite so well as the Morris Minor – in fact, the little car was as far ahead of its competition in this respect as would be the Mini some eleven years later.

Morris' great rival, Austin, was also developing a small saloon – the A30 (later the A35) which, although a successful car, was not to enjoy the long production life – spanning four decades – of the Minor. The A30 was smaller and more economical on fuel than the Minor, thanks in part to its lighter weight but to a large extent to its Weslake overhead valve A series engine. The Minor was stuck with an old-fashioned sidevalve unit which was not only less attractive in terms of fuel economy than the OHV A series engine, but also gave a very sluggish performance.

In the early 1950s the British Motor Corporation was formed. BMC was an amalgamation of a large chunk of the British motor manufacturing industry – but was essentially a merging of the Austin and Morris companies. One very positive side-effect of the merger was that the Minor was fitted with the far better A series engine, which gave it a quite creditable performance for the period. The merger also – more importantly – brought together Alec Issigonis and the A series engine, a double act destined to produce the most influential new car of all time.

The post-war petrol shortage was to be exacerbated in the mid-1950s by the Suez crisis, leading to rationing and bringing about an urgent need for even more fuel-efficient full four seater saloons. The best BMC had to offer was the Austin A30 range which, although economical, was very cramped in the back, suitable in reality only for seating children: the Minor was by far the better car in this respect, but at the cost of larger external dimensions and extra weight which of course meant slightly higher fuel consumption.

The problem was how to fit a quart into a pint pot. Seating four adults in any degree of comfort took a fixed amount of volume, but a considerable amount of the available internal volume of the small car was already taken up with a transmission tunnel which usually swelled around the gearbox. Another intrusion into the available passenger volume was inevitably the rear chassis rail/heelboard assembly – then more or less a standard feature of monocoque car body construction which was necessary in order to soak up the stresses imposed by rear wheel drive. Under or behind the rear seats, a lot of room was needed to accommodate the rear axle, differential casing, plus its range of vertical movement. If this lost internal volume could be recovered, the external dimensions of a car could be reduced without compromising passenger volume – the question was, how?

At the same time, the engine naturally took up a considerable amount of space under the bonnet, but on most cars there was a lot of unused volume either side of the engine. Issigonis solved all of these problems with one brilliant concept; the transversely-mounted engine, with integral gearbox driving the front wheels. The car was Austin Development Office (ADO) 15.

The transmission tunnel which, on rear wheel drive cars had to accommodate not only the propeller shaft but also its range of vertical movement, could be reduced to a vestigial swage whose only purpose was to help stiffen the floorpan. There was no intrusion because of an axle casing, no need for great structural strength in the form of a massive heelboard assembly or rear chassis legs.

Turning the engine through ninety degrees was only part of the story – Issigonis also identified unused volume in the engine oil sump, so situated the gearbox in the sump with the differential bolted onto the new casing. This permitted the length of the engine bay to be reduced to little more than the width of the engine; and so reduced the overall length of the car to produce what must surely, even today, be recognised as the ideal car for use in town.

More space saving came in the suspension. Both coil and leaf spring suspensions took up too much volume for Mr Issigonis' liking; Alex Moulton (of bicycle fame) helped to develop a suspension based on rubber cones in place of steel springs. This was built into two detachable subframes – one front, one rear – which themselves performed those functions normally associated with the chassis members of rear wheel drive monocoque cars.

There was a plan at one stage during the Mini's development to fit a two-stroke twin cylinder engine, but with the Suez crisis by then fading away and with petrol no longer rationed, the smoothness, tractability and availability of the tried and trusted A series engine made it the obvious choice.

There was a perhaps unexpected or certainly under-estimated bonus which came with Issigonis' space-saving design – by virtue of its front wheel drive and having 'a wheel at each corner', the Mini held the road better than any other production saloon car of the time. Like Issigonis' Minor before it, the Mini set new standards in road-holding.

Prior to the Mini's launch, BMC were so confident of the Mini's ability to go around corners better than anything else on four wheels that they did not have to tell anyone how good the car was, they merely had to let motoring scribes sample it for themselves. A great Press event was organised in which a fleet of cars was put through its paces by the leading motoring journalists of the day. Everyone loved it; a few may have been aware that they were witnessing a new era in car design.

In 1959, ADO 15 was unveiled to the public – badged both as the Morris Mini Minor and Austin Se7en. It was – surprisingly – not an instant success but, following well-publicised purchases by a growing band of nobility and celebrities which raised public awareness of the Mini and made it chic to be seen in, sales began to seriously take off.

Everybody who was anybody, as the saying goes, in the 1960s London which was then fashion Capital of the World, owned a Mini. The celebrities were generally photographed receiving their new Minis, and thereafter the papers and magazines were full of photographs of them getting into their Minis, out of their Minis, driving, parking, sitting in, leaning against; in the petrol station, in Town for the evening, leaving the theatre – the Mini became the most photographed car. For the Smart Set, the Mini became a vital fashion accessory.

But the Mini was increasingly finding favour with the motoring public for an entirely different set of reasons. It was cheap to run, cheap to maintain but above all, it was great fun to drive despite its 'mere' 850cc engine and 34bhp (which was not an untypical power output for a small car at the time). It wasn't what the Mini had, it was the way that it used it. On typically winding country roads, journey times came down for those driving a Mini. It took a long time to wind an 850 Mini up to any sort of speed but, once there, you could maintain that speed and let the front wheels pull you around bends which forced the drivers of most rear wheel drive cars to brake furiously, cog down and then floor the throttle as they exited in a vain effort to keep up.

In slippery conditions, especially in snow, the Mini was second only to four wheel drive vehicles. If the front wheels lost traction, see-saw on the steering wheel and they soon dug down and found something to grip. But there was a 'down' side to the roadholding excellence of the Mini.

Inexperienced drivers with little skill but big ambitions were able to go faster in a Mini than they could have in any contemporary car, but the well-behaved Mini did not, unlike rear wheel drive cars, scream warnings at them to slow down as they approached the limits of adhesion – it just suddenly let go.

A lot of Minis perished at the hands of over-enthusiastic but under-experienced drivers.

COMPETITION

The most skilled of drivers, however, could read the Minis on-road feedback, and after Pat Moss won the Mille Miglia rally in 1959 in a standard production Morris Mini Minor, the potential for the Mini in motorsport became apparent to all. Against the wishes of Issigonis – who insisted that the Mini was for nurses rather than racing drivers – John Cooper persuaded the company to let him take one Mini for development into a performance car – the first Mini Cooper – which bore fruit in September of 1961. The pudding stirrer gearshift lever was replaced with a short remote unit (making use of the vestigial 'transmission tunnel'), the engine was enlarged to a capacity of 997cc which, coupled with a twin-carb induction, raised power from 34bhp to 55bhp.

Although the Mini today is remembered largely for its celebrated 1960s rally successes, the 1961 British Saloon Car Championship saw the first in a series of track victories; the Mini was also outright victor in the BSCC in 1962 and 1966, against formidable opposition, most notably from vast and powerful American saloons.

On the rally front, in 1962 Pat Moss again drove the Mini to victory, scoring outright wins in both the Baden-Baden and Tulip rallies. BMC had a stab at the Big rally – the Monte Carlo – in 1960, '61, '62 and '63, and in 1964 Paddy Hopkirk drove a Cooper S registered 33 EJB to outright victory in the Monte.

In 1965, Timo Makinen repeated the exercise, and the Mini Cooper S in fact scored outright wins in a great many prestigious international rallies, including the Circuit of Ireland, Geneva, Czechoslovakian, Polish, 1,000 Lakes, Munich-Vienna-Bucharest and – not least – the RAC.

In 1966, the Mini Cooper came in first, second, third (and a Lotus Cortina came in fourth) in the Monte Carlo but, by this time, (arguably over-patriotic) race officials had had enough of cars built by their own countrymen being trounced by Minis and disqualified the lot on a technicality so tenuous that it is difficult to consider it anything other than trumped-up – 'it' being that the headlamp dipping arrangements were illegal.

Far from being despondent at the disqualification, the British people appear to have recognised the fact that the car had scored the double triumph of not only trouncing the rest of the field but also severely unhinging certain of the opposition. The cars and drivers – Makinen, Aaltonen and Hopkirk in first, second and third places respectively, were fêted on their return to Blighty with as much gusto as if the genuine results had stood.

Undisputed wins in 1966 included the Circuit of Ireland, Tulip, Austrian Alpine, Scottish, Czechoslovakian, Polish, 1,000 lakes and Munich-Vienna-Budapest.

In 1967 the Mini Cooper again romped home to take the Monte Carlo, and won a clutch of other international rallies. In the following year, BMC became British Leyland and the Mini Cooper's days as the World's top rally car were coming to an end.

The Mini Cooper ceased production in 1971, to be replaced by the 1275GT which, due to the preparation and driving skills of Richard Longman, took overall first in the British Saloon Car Championship in both 1978 and 1979. Despite out-selling the Coopers, the 1275GT could never replace them in the hearts of die-hard Mini fans, and it was not until the late 1980s that classic enthusiasts began to realise what a good little car it really was.

PRODUCTION

While the Mini Coopers were dominating the world rally scene, the standard Mini was constantly being revamped and revised. Capitalising, perhaps, on the long-term success enjoyed by the Morris Minor Traveller, the Mk.1 Mini Countryman appeared in 1960 – unlike the

33 EJB was driven to outright victory by Paddy Hopkirk in the 1964 Monte Carlo – 21 years later, Paddy drove L33 EJB in the 1995 event.

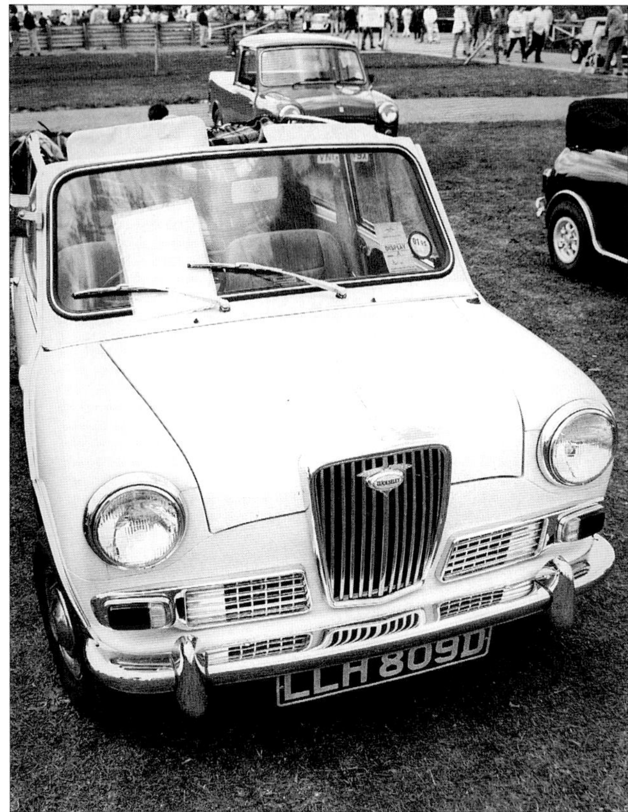

A Wolseley Hornet is quite a rare sight nowadays; convertibles are very scarce – this one was photographed at the Mini 35 celebrations.

Also seen at Mini 35, this early Cooper convertible.

Minor Traveller possessing only non-structural decorative woodwork.

The Mini van – workhorse of countless thousands of small businesses – also appeared in 1960 and found favour not least because of its comparatively huge carrying capacity in so small a package. The rear subframe and radius arm/rubber cone suspension which took far less internal volume than an axle and differential casing meant that the Mini van had a low rear floor and was therefore easy to load. Couple this with economy and tenacious road-holding, and it's little wonder that the Mini van was such a success. The following year, it was joined by the pick-up.

In 1961 the Mini story took a new twist with the introduction of the Wolseley Hornet and Riley Elf. Up-market badges for an up-market Mini, with part-leather upholstery, a 998cc engine, stubby rear wings flanking an enlarged boot. You could buy a new Mini wearing a classy badge and with a bit of luxury, 60s style, and increased luggage capacity, up to 1969.

The first 997cc Mini Cooper, introduced in

Australian Moke at a meeting of Worcester Mini club. The owner carried out all restoration work save the painting himself.

The driver and passenger in a Moke must be on friendly terms – they quite literally rub shoulders!

1961, was replaced in 1964 by the 998cc version, which ran till 1967. The Cooper S as launched in 1963, featured a 1071cc engine and found fame as a rally winner. In 1964 and 5, a 970cc engine was fitted, and in 1965 the definitive Cooper S – the 1275 – was launched. The Cooper and Cooper S went into Mk.2 guise along with the standard car in 1967.

In 1964 the Mini Moke was introduced, offered to the military without success (the lack of four-wheel drive didn't help, but it was almost certainly the lack of ground clearance which killed any chance the Moke might have had to sell to the forces), and four years later with numbers under 30,000, the Moke ceased UK production. The Moke was rather better received overseas in warmer climes, and was manufactured in Australia and to this day in Portugal by Casiva.

In 1965, the one millionth Mini rolled from the production line – a big media event, but this production milestone was inexplicably not – unlike the Morris Minor before it – marked with a special limited edition car. Pity.

The Mk.2 Mini was in this author's opinion a real 'curate's egg' of a car. At last, the standard car got a remote gearshift, though engine capacity stayed at 848cc and the car was fitted with hydrolastic suspension which softened the ride but took away some of the Minis sporty feel. In 1969, however, the option of a 998cc engine (Mini 1000), coupled with a suspension which reverted back to rubber cone, meant that the car had a more fitting power output for the 1970s plus the original sporty ride.

The Mini 1000 was introduced along with the Clubman, Clubman Estate and 1275GT in October of 1969. Whereas the standard shape Mini had thankfully reverted to dry suspension,

The Clubman might not be everybody's favourite Mini, but a nice example is very covetable.

the Clubman range – including the mildly sporting 1275GT – had hydrolastic suspension. These too went 'dry' in 1971.

Clubman front-end styling is something of an acquired taste which relatively few Mini fans appear to appreciate. Access to the engine bay for maintenance is slightly improved over the standard car, but any feelings of security courtesy of the extra steel out front are probably more imagined than real.

In November of 1969, the two millionth Mini was produced – one eighth of that total during the year in question. Still no limited edition car to mark this milestone.

The three millionth and four millionth Minis were produced in 1972 and 1976 respectively and still no special edition. Even in the midst of the special-edition rich 1980s, the five millionth Mini was not marked with its own commemorative special edition. It seems inexplicable, after the eighties proved a decade in which anything and everything was celebrated by a Special Limited Edition Mini, that such fundamental milestones were apparently not capitalised upon.

Back, as they say, to the plot. Throughout the 1970s, Mini production chugged along, well after – some feared – its 'sell-by' date. With the exception of the limited edition Mini 1000 of October 1975, there were a number of small changes here and there such as alternators across the range in '73, ditto heaters in '74, but no change of real substance until the 850 was finally discontinued in July of 1979 after twenty years' continuous production. The rather quick 1100 Special limited edition (5000 produced with metallic silver or rose paintwork – a classic if you can find a straight one) was introduced the same year.

Throughout the late 1970s and into the early 1980s, British Leyland suffered worsening industrial disruption which, allied to sometimes questionable quality control and a less than inspiring range of cars, made the state-owned manufacturer a great drain on the public purse. A Canadian, Graham Day, was appointed by Prime Minister Margaret Thatcher to sort things out. Some predicted the end of the line for the Mini.

In fact, the Mini was one of the very few profitable Leyland cars of the time, despite having been the Cinderella of the range when it came to advertising and promotion. Graham (now Sir Graham) Day encouraged the concept of Limited Edition Minis, and was also the driving force behind the famous 'Minis have feelings too' advertising campaign, which helped to increase sales of the Mini by keeping the car in the public eye.

The Mini Clubman shape became history in 1980, and the standard Mini remained in the market place, selling both on its merits and increasingly due to its cult and classic car status. The classic car movement was at the time starting to grow, as more and more of the post-war generation realised that the few remaining examples of cars of their youth were now desirable classics – worth restoring and then keeping for the fun of the occasional outing. The only such car still to be in production was the Mini. Little wonder that the various limited and special edition Minis found such a ready and lucrative market.

Although the Mini 1000 Special of 1975, the 1100 Special of 1979 and Sprite (2,500 made) of 1983 all sold well, the real run of Mini specials started with the 25th Anniversary 'Silver Jubilee' limited edition of 1984, of which 5,000 were made. The company organised the second Mini 'Birthday Party' at Donnington – the first such event having been the 21st party, held at Brands Hatch. The fact that the Mini was 25 years old made news, the publicity drove interest in the limited edition car, and the company realised that niche marketing was a viable proposition long before other car manufacturers took up the idea in the late 1980s.

The Mini Ritz (3,725 cars) was followed by the Chelsea (1,500 cars), Piccadilly (2,500 cars) and Park Lane (1,500 cars) – what might be considered the 'London' collection in years to come! The names of specials then flew off at a tangent.

The Mini Advantage was launched in the midst of the tennis season in 1987, and the production run was 2,500. This was arguably the first 'designer' Mini – a very 1980s phenomenon – colour-coded from its Diamond white paintwork down to its jade green pinstripes and tennis ball logo.

In 1986, Graham Day changed the name of the company from British Leyland to Rover – a new name for the turned-around company to help bury the ties with its troubled recent past. Also in 1986, Kevin Morley was appointed Managing Director.

In 1988 the Jet Black and Red Hot specials were unveiled (2,000 cars), followed by the Mini Designer, which featured designs by Mary Quant (also 2,000 cars). The designer trend quietly dying towards the end of the yuppie decade heralded a revival of 1960s styles and values, rekindled in two of the limited edition quartet – Flame, Racing (2,000 cars), Rose and Sky (1,000 cars) – the first two in traditional red and British Racing Green livery respectively, the latter a continuation of the designer theme in white with a pink or blue roof.

Then in 1989 came the Mini Thirty (3,000 cars). Obviously, linked to a huge Mini celebration, this special was certain to attract much media and hence public attention. The third 'Birthday Party' was organised at Silverstone and attracted 130,000 people, 37,000 Minis turning up on the day.

The Flame and Racing were re-introduced in 1990, along with the Checkmate (black paintwork, white roof), and 2,500 of these were sold. Also in 1990, 2,000 examples of the Mini Studio 2 were produced. But the Big Event of 1990 was yet to come…

John Cooper (he of Mini Cooper fame) had for some time been retailing a conversion kit

The rather tasty Mini Marcos has been around for years, and is covetable to this day.

To anyone interested in motorsport (or even cars in general) who grew up in the 1960s, the name 'Mini Cooper' is probably one of the most evocative. Little wonder that when, in 1990, a limited edition of 1,000 Mini Coopers was announced, the production run was snapped up in very short time! The Cooper thereafter became a standard Rover Mini production model.

through his business, John Cooper Garages and, in 1990, the first 1,000 new Mini Coopers were announced as a limited edition – all of which were sold very quickly, and some of which were immediately re-advertised (delivery mileage only) at hugely inflated prices by some speculators who bought them. The Mini

Several of the Limited Edition Minis had the R26 radio as standard equipment. It is interesting to note that the original Mini design did not allow for a radio mounting space – because Alec Issigonis didn't like radios! Truly, that first design was the vision of one man.

Cooper was the first Mini for ten years to be fitted with the 1275cc engine, and continued in production as a standard part of the range.

Tightening exhaust emissions regulations were introduced which could only be satisfactorily addressed by fitting catalytic converters, which obviously threatened the future of the Mini, but the Mini was indeed fitted with cats – both carburettor versions and those with the more appropriate fuel injection.

Meanwhile, the specials continued unabated. The Neon (1,500 cars) of 1991 was followed by a beautiful convertible special from LAMM Autohaus (75 cars – priced at £12,250 – sold out in the first week). 1992 saw the introduction of the Italian Job, 1993 the Rio, the production Cabriolet, and limited edition Tahiti, and in 1994 the Mini 35 Special Edition, to celebrate 35 years of Mini production.

The fourth Birthday Party for the Mini at Silverstone will not be forgotten by those who attended it. One and a half hours to travel the last eight miles to the circuit – the 100,000-plus attendance meant that there were queues to get in, queues to get out, queues to get anywhere – I know, I was there. I had secured a press pass, and found myself standing out on the balcony where the winner's podium was situated, in the company of such luminaries as Paddy Hopkirk and Bernd Pischetsrieder (Chairman of BMW – Rover's new and, as time would tell – benevolent – parent company).

Contrary to the scare stories which circulated

A line-up of Minis ready to entertain the crowds at the 35th birthday party.

in the motoring press following the BMW takeover, Mini was not axed – in fact, Bernd Pischetsrieder is a self-confessed classic car enthusiast with, I suspect, a soft spot for the Mini Cooper. BMW allowed executives to choose Rover or BMW cars as their company vehicles, and it is reported that in addition to Range Rovers and Land Rovers, Minis are to be seen in the BMW car park! With such estimable friends in high places, Mini looks set to remain the Great British Survivor for some time to come.

Someone – possibly Rover PR staff – plucked this chap (with Mini on the brain) from the crowd at the Mini 35th birthday party.

SURVIVE BUYING YOUR MINI

I hate buying cars. I hate it because there's so much to see – so much to take in – that my mind has a tendency to go completely blank. I wander around the car aimlessly, looking but not seeing. If, on the other hand, I'm looking at a car on someone else's behalf then nothing gets past me – not even the tiniest detail. Just to prove the point, I went out yesterday to look at a recent Mini limited edition, on sale at a local dealer's – kidding myself that I was looking on someone else's behalf.

Almost at once I noticed rust staining around the front offside body seam cover which, on this recent car, indicated that it had

at some point been taken off, possibly during collision damage repair. Within a couple of minutes, I had found Mig weld at the top of the offside windscreen pillar and freshly-painted filler on the bulkhead under the offside scuttle – side impact. There was more freshly-painted filler on the nearside flitch front. This car had been hit gently on the nearside front and had sustained rather more serious damage to the offside – I find such problems immediately when I'm looking for someone else. What's more, I find myself drawn as if by magic straight to the car's problem areas, and can rule out most ineligible cars at a glance. And that's another reason why I hate buying cars – the majority on the second-hand market fail to meet my standards.

The wording of advertisements is often misleading. You can travel miles to view a car advertised as 'restored' for example, only to discover at first sight that it has had large helpings of bodyfiller crudely plastered over obvious rust spots and been given a respray of such poor quality that the surface of the paint has a texture like that of sandpaper. You might alternatively view a nearly-new car advertised as being in excellent condition, only to raise the bonnet and find a crumpled flitch panel which tells of a front-end shunt. This does not necessarily mean that the vendors are crooked, many will be selling their cars genuinely unaware of such problems. Don't travel miles and miles to view Minis – you'll have plenty of wasted journeys, so look only at cars near to home.

Better still, make your way to the nearest specialist Mini dealer – you'll be able to view many Minis at the cost of a single journey. Plus you've some redress if the car you buy turns out to be less than you expected. In addition, Mini dealers should be experienced enough to avoid the lemons – let the dealers wear their tyres out tracking down good Minis, and you can save a lot of time and effort at the cost of the dealer's mark-up.

You should face the fact that a car is offered for sale because its owner did not want it. In many cases, there will be a perfectly plausible reason for this, such as raising funds for some pressing need, a change in circumstances – redundancy, extra baby on the way and so on. In many cases, however, the car will be on the market because it is less than perfect.

I hate buying cars.

NEW MINIS

At the time of writing, many new small cars have reduced in price, leaving the Mini somewhat stranded and oft-criticised by the motoring press for being over-priced for what it offers. That is fine if you consider only the equipment level, luggage space, raw performance figures and general refinement. But today's Mini buyer attaches little importance to such matters, because he or she wants not a new modern 'Supermini' – but a new Mini – and if the ride is a little harsher, the interior arguably less spacious and less comfortable, the luggage capacity less and the 0-60mph time a little longer than the competition – that's all for the good, because these are the very traits which make the 1990s Mini different from today's upstarts.

Most of the people who read this book will harbour dreams of one day acquiring a brand-new Mini – even the 'classic' Mini enthusiast will be sorely tempted to add a new example to his or her collection – and there will always be that nagging doubt that if we don't move and buy one now, we might miss the chance for ever if the car ceases production. One thing seems certain – if (when) the end of the line is announced for the Mini, Rover are going to be deluged with orders for the last few cars! However, British Heritage – a division of Rover which has for a few years been re-manufacturing shells for the MGB, Midget and TR6 – are almost certain to be the recipients of the Mini body panel press tools and other specialist tools when the Mini production eventually ends, so those who showed the foresight to buy a 1990s Mini will hopefully be well served with top-quality spares for many a year to come and the Mini – we hope – will live on in the hands of enthusiasts.

Buying a new Mini is easy. Go to your local Rover dealer, write out a cheque and drive away in your new Mini confident that the car is 100% roadworthy. Your only decisions are which model to buy, whether you might wait for the next limited edition car and what colour. I wish that I had such problems!

While it seems that every motor manufacturer is today launching tarted-up limited edition variants of their mainstream cars, every Mini special which comes to the market is in an altogether higher class. In my opinion, every Mini is a classic car in its own right and, if a Mini happens to be one of a limited edition, it is to many even more desirable as a classic than is the standard issue.

With limited production runs typically averaging between 1,000 and 3,000, and with exports (especially to Japan) eating up a large chunk of each, the best advice for anyone wanting a limited edition car is to contact your local Rover dealer and declare your interest in the next limited edition. This should be sufficient for the dealer to be motivated to contact you the moment the new edition is announced to the trade and, should you decide that you cannot live with the colour scheme of the new car, you're under no obligation because you have not placed a firm order.

Even a base model Sprite of 1995 is a classic, but unlike most classic cars it has the extra virtue of being brand new. Older Minis become progressively more desirable as classics, newer cars progressively more desirable as reliable fun transport – the Mini, uniquely, scores both ways!

USED MINIS

Before setting out on what will probably become the first of many wild goose chases in search of the Mini of your dreams, it is best to sit down and decide exactly what you are looking for – variant, age, condition and price. After seeing a few cars you might well wish to revise this, on the grounds that most of the examples on the market were in too poor condition, overpriced, or whatever. Don't set yourself any kind of deadline, either, because if you buy in haste then in my bitter experience you'll always regret having done so.

The main priorities when looking for any used Mini are (in order of importance)...

1. Is the car being offered for sale legally?
2. Check for collision damage, which may be camouflaged.
3. Check for bodyrot, which may also be camouflaged.
4. Check major mechanical/electrical units.
5. How well has the car been maintained?

The used car market is and always has been a jungle – venture into it alone only if you have real survival skills. Otherwise, find yourself an expert to guide you.

I have seen some older – pre 1980s – Minis offered for sale on the open market which were best described not so much as 'unroadworthy' but as being close to death traps. Dampers which were seized solid or filled with a mixture of mud and water, rear subframes bolted onto rotten heelboards, bodyshells which were bent so that the cars crabbed along and roadholding anywhere near the limit could be lethal, deficiencies in the braking and steering, damaged wire insulation capable of starting an electrical fire. Even such glaring faults as seized dampers, rotten subframes and bald tyres. Some of these cars may be offered with an MOT.

How do patently unroadworthy cars acquire an MOT certificate? There are a number of ways – all of them illegal. Happily, the days of the 'bent' tester appear to be over – spot checks and testing by Ministry officials make MOT skulduggery a dangerous business. Bent MOT testers might be a dying breed, but theft of blank certificates appears to be a growing industry and blank MOT certificates are highly prized by, and sometimes feature in the hauls of burglars, who know that there is always a ready market for them. Some unscrupulous vendors might bring their cars to MOT standard by fitting new dampers, brake shoes and so on, but swap these for the illegal originals once the certificate has been written out. Out and out villains can use a 'ringer' – a similar Mini wearing the number plates and identification plates of one which could never acquire an MOT on its own merit.

WMOC ERA. Your local Mini owners' club is the best place to see a variety of Minis and so choose which variant is for you. This Worcester MOC meeting included the ERA, an Australian Moke, a Minus kit car and my British Classic.

The fact must be faced that a current MOT certificate actually tells you nothing about the condition or roadworthiness of a car. You have to take steps yourself to determine whether a Mini you are offered is roadworthy or lethal. Unless you possess extensive knowledge and are able to assess the mechanical components and bodywork, you are strongly advised to either have the car MOT tested by a business you know and trust (ask the tester to also check for signs of bodyrot and collision damage after the 'official' test), to pay a professional mechanic or restorer to check the car over for you, or to commission a motor engineer's report.

Given that a car is in sound and roadworthy condition, you next have to establish that the vendor is in a legal position to sell the car to

Look along external panelwork, moving your head as you do so, and noting whether the reflection distorts, indicating dents, poor bodyfiller finishing, etc.

Small cracks in the windscreen seal have probably been caused during its removal and replacement. You can affect a repair of sorts using windscreen sealant, but a new rubber is the only really satisfactory solution.

you. This requires that he or she actually owns the car, and that no other person or body (such as a finance company, most obviously) has any title or claim on it in the form of outstanding repayments on a loan.

In the case of recent one-owner cars, the vendor should be able to show you the original bill of sale from the dealer, which is easily validated. Most of the cars on the second hand market have had many owners, and are not so easily checked. A receipt from the previous owner of the car should be made available for your inspection, and you may be able to contact the person named to ensure that everything is above board, although this is far from proof positive that the car is legitimate. Ask to see current and previous paperwork – tax discs, insurance documentation, MOT certificates – because the rightful owner of the car *should* be

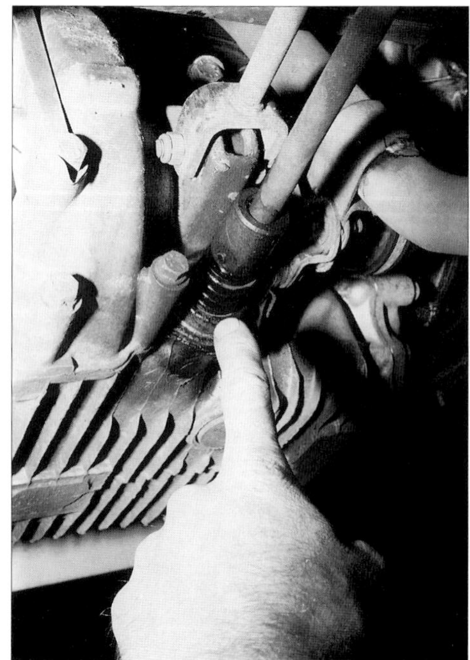

Small oil leaks such as this one from the gear selector shaft oil seal are by no means uncommon. Some result in MOT failure. All need rectifying.

able to furnish these, whereas the vendor of a stolen car won't. In the UK, the best bet if everything seems in order at this stage is to then contact HPI Autodata (tel. 01722 422422) who, for a fee, will check its records to ascertain whether the car is registered as an insurance write-off, stolen or the subject of outstanding finance. If you can pay by credit card then HPI will give you an answer there and then – otherwise, you'll have to wait until they post you the information in writing. Written confirmation follows all enquiries. HPI cannot guarantee that their records are 100% correct and up to date but, in the absence of any better service, it is highly recommended. If you have trouble contacting HPI, or are outside the UK, the police should be able to tell you how to contact a similar service.

If you have established that the car is in good condition, and are convinced that there is nothing illegal about its sale, don't rush in and buy it – take all the time you like to make your mind up. Are you really happy with the car and – equally importantly – with the vendor? If you have any misgivings about either, even tiny nagging doubts which you cannot articulate, then look elsewhere. We've all seen used car advertisements which include the bitter words "Re-advertised due to time-waster" – *be* that time-waster. Take all the time you like and, if you're not 100% comfortable with the car and seller, walk away. One of the most important points to bear in mind when buying a Mini is that there are a lot of Minis about – if you miss this one while dilly-dallying then another, better example is sure to turn up sooner or later.

Also remember that many people decide to sell their cars because they know something you don't – that expensive problems are looming, or perhaps the car is for whatever reason unreliable or un-roadworthy. The vendor should be able to give you a convincing reason for the car's being offered for sale – if not, don't give them the benefit of the doubt – decline to buy the car and walk away.

If you suspect that the clutch is on the way out, bear in mind that it is not an easy item to replace, but that any professional mechanic should be able to do the job in maybe two hours – subtract two hours' labour charge plus the cost of a clutch from the asking price.

This sort of thing doesn't inspire much confidence – the radius arm grease nipple has not received much attention, and the rest of the car will probably prove similarly neglected.

If the oil clinging to the end of the dipstick smells of petrol, this – the mechanical fuel pump – is the culprit. A replacement pump is not terribly expensive, and earlier ones can be repaired – getting the pump off the engine, however, is a very time-consuming job so, if the oil smells of petrol, perhaps you can ask the vendor to have the work done before you buy the car.

The engine number should be on a plate here.

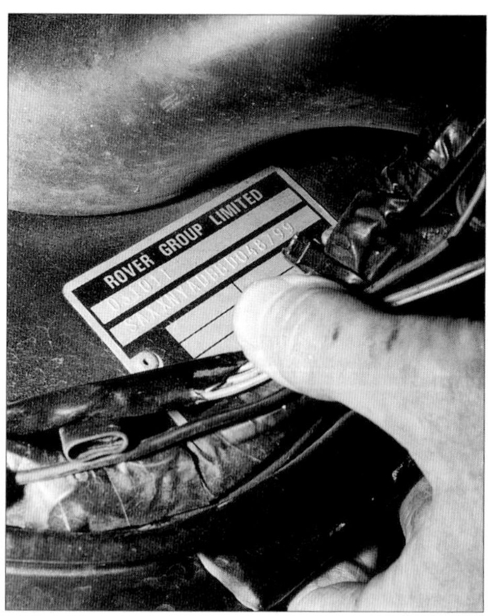

The Vehicle Identification Number (VIN).

One sure sign that the vendor knows of problems or looming problems with the car is when he or she watches you like a hawk when you're trying to appraise the car. If the vendor suddenly draws your attention away from an area you are viewing, you can bet that you are getting pretty close to finding said fault.

Never be hurried by the vendor into making a decision: if the vendor indicates that there is a lot of interest in the car, that someone else is almost certain to buy it if you don't – then it's probably best to walk away.

I have discovered that the best mental approach when viewing cars is to firstly convince myself that I have no intention of buying it, that I'm only going for a look, that the car will almost certainly prove over-priced and that I will find fault with it. Go with this attitude and you'll find it easier to reject the car without suffering nagging doubts that you could be missing a bargain.

When assessing a used Mini you should look especially for signs of bodyrot – which is often camouflaged – and for signs of collision damage. A rotten or bent old Mini is only worth whatever can be raised when it has been broken up for spares, yet many people (including me) have unsuspectingly bought such unroadworthy cars in the past.

To find bodyrot and camouflaged bodyrot, look at the toeboard, heelboard and the rear part of the front inner wheelarch (all can be seen from inside the car – the heelboard ends are under the back seat base and can be seen with a torch for illumination). Still inside the car, remove the rear glove pocket liners and look at the visible portion of the sill structure and the inside of the quarter panel, and lift the carpets or mats and look for GRP or bodyfiller anywhere on the floorpan/sill assembly. If you find GRP, reject the car, because if it's bodged here, expect the same elsewhere.

On the outside, use a magnet to check for thick bodyfiller on the roof pillars and roof (the car has been rolled and is probably bent) in the top scuttle ends (bottom corners of the windscreen), the A panel, quarter panel and boot floor – in other words, the entire topside of the car!

The 'A' post contains the door hinges, and is often bodged. Happily, the usual give-away for this is the amount of vertical play of the door, so open it then try to raise it – a little play can sometimes be put down to worn hinges, but you might see the whole A post moving with it!

Finding uncorrected or poorly 'repaired' crash damage is equally important. Damage is usually apparent as *rivelling* – that is, corrugations or undulations in panels which should be flat. It is normal for the paint to crack when a panel becomes rivelled, and this will be apparent as a number of straight lines of rust, especially in the flitch panels. More obvious clues such as poorly fitting doors, bonnet and boot lid should not be overlooked. Check for rivelling in the toeboard and floorpan inside the car, the flitch panels (inner wings) in the engine bay, the boot floor and the inner rear wings.

While rivelling indicates collision damage, it does not necessarily prove that the car has sustained collision damage heavy enough to have bent it – to have pushed one or both subframes out of alignment. However, unless you especially want that particular car (i.e. it is a rare variant, or exactly the year, colour etc. that you crave) my advice is to reject the car. Even if it is basically straight, those rivelled panels will rot out more quickly than will the rest of the car, and they are, once damaged, not up to full strength. If you absolutely must have that car, then get it checked out by a motor engineer, who should be able to prove/disprove whether it is straight or bent.

Mechanically, an old Mini can range from well-maintained examples which offer tens of thousands of miles' trouble-free motoring to neglected unreliable heaps which never want to start in the morning and which break down with monotonous regularity. A Mini which is really poor mechanically (and with regard to the electrics) can cost more to keep on the road over a number of years than would be needed to fund a professional bodywork restoration! Such cars might be cheap to buy, but in the long run they'll cost a fortune.

This is the sort of heelboard patch repair you need to be on your guard against. Such a repair will usually be disguised inside the car with bodyfiller, so check the heelboard ends using a magnet and, if you find ANY filler, reject the car.

Heelboard end under seat. On recent Minis, you might find evidence of heavy rear collision under the rear seat base (though it's unlikely). Look here on older cars; the heelboard ends rot out and the rear subframe is bolted on not a million miles away. If you find body-filler or any signs of damage here, I'd reject the car, because this is not an easy repair.

Liner under the glove compartment. Lift out the cardboard liner, and you can see the true state of the sill ends.

You should look firstly for signs that the car has been properly maintained, which means a clean engine bay, recent ignition components and oil filter. The engine oil level should be correct, and the oil should not be thick and black, nor should you discover a yellow-ochre gunge inside the rocker box cover (water in the oil – commonly caused by condensation on cars used predominantly for short journeys, but also possibly caused by a damaged head gasket or a cracked cylinder head or block). If you discover evidence of water in the oil, check out the coolant – if this contains traces of oil (which floats to the surface in the radiator filler cap) then budget for a new head gasket, cylinder head or even, if the block is cracked – engine. The wiring loom should not have any lengths of wire with discoloured insulation. The fan belt, steering rack gaiters and engine hoses etc. should be in good condition, as should the tyres.

If the service book is still valid then a full set of service stamps is a good sign (but always check with the garage concerned that the work has actually been carried out).

Generally, unless you are already experienced enough to be able to adjudge the condition of a car then I strongly recommend that you enlist the assistance of someone who is. A mechanic from your local garage might be persuaded to give the car a once-over for a small fee; alternatively, book the car in for an MOT and ask the tester to be especially scrupulous (this will astound him – people usually want the opposite!). Most motoring organizations will – for a fee – check cars for members; independent

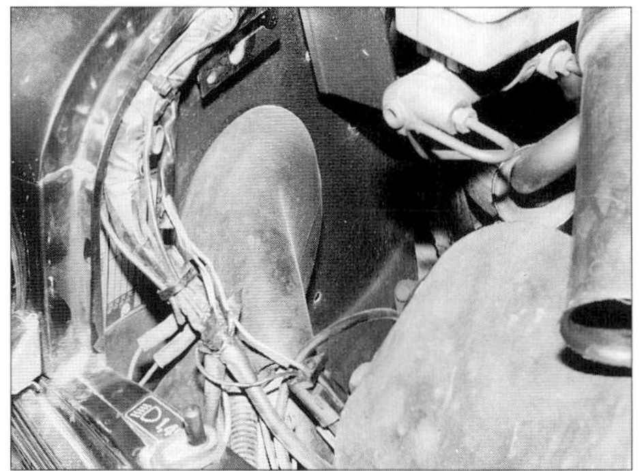

Flitch. Front wings, although welded into place, are not too difficult to replace, but the flitch is another matter, so even if the wings are perfect, take a look at the flitch panels – especially the very front – rivelling indicates heavy collision.

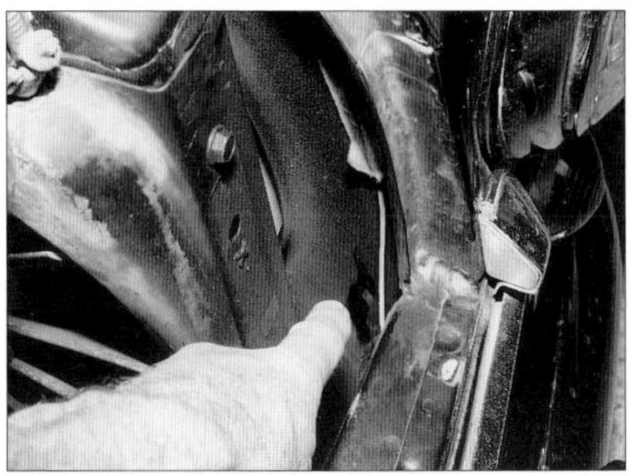

Flitch near side. The nearside of the Mini engine bay is remarkably crowded, and it's difficult to see much of the flitch. The lower leading edge is always the first to suffer during a collision, so look here at least.

On this car, the flitch panels have been replaced, following a front-end shunt of some magnitude. The give-away is the welding on the bracing panels.

motor engineers will do the same and are listed in local trade telephone directories and – last but by no means least – your local Mini Owners' Club may well have a member sufficiently experienced and friendly enough to check a car on your behalf.

A full guide to appraising Minis is included in the book *Mini – Restoration/ Preparation/ Maintenance*, £19.99, published by Osprey, (author, erm, Jim Tyler). Buyers' guides also appear periodically in classic car magazines.

The same car. While the clutch was being attended to, I noticed that the spot welded join between the flitch and the wing top was less than perfect – just the sort of give-away clue you should be looking for when assessing a car.

On older cars, expect flitch panel surface rusting. To clean the flitch back to bare steel and repaint it entails firstly removing the engine and radiator – a lot of work.

LATE MINIS

Recent Minis might appear the safest of buys, but any Mini other than a brand new one can at some time in its life have been written off or 'bent' in an unrecorded (insurance-wise) accident. The Mini has two things going against it in this respect. Firstly, it is rightly a very popular learners' and inexperienced drivers' 'first' car, being easy to drive, cheap to run and insure. Secondly, inexperienced drivers being lulled by the sure-footed roadholding of the Mini means that when they have their first road accident, it can be a relatively high-speed one. The net result is that quite a few Minis have been written off.

In theory, insurance write-offs should be scrapped or, at the very least, straightened on a jig and have all the bent panels replaced. But many have been tarted up – complete with bodyshell distortion – and sold on to unsuspecting buyers.

A motor engineer should be able to spot a bent Mini a mile off, but few Mini buyers consider spending what can be a sizeable proportion of the asking price of a used Mini on a

ANY repair involving a component situated at the back of the Mini engine is a pain – to replace the down pipe or fuel pump, it is best to begin by removing the carburettor.

Staining like this is left when antifreeze evaporates. Check not only the radiator, but also hose junctions. This staining could well have been spillage when topping up the radiator.

Take a peek in the rocker box cover. If you see a yellowish sludge then the oil has mixed with water to produce said emulsion. Could be due to too many short trips (condensation) or possibly cylinder head or gasket problems. Find out which.

Advanced gunge – actually, the engine is out of an 1968 Minor, but even fairly recent cars used mainly for short trips can become like this. It needs flushing during the engine oil change.

motor engineer's report. A couple of quick checks might help weed out bent cars. Firstly, unless the tyres are new, look at the tread wear on the rear tyres – if this is not even, it could be down to worn radius arm bearings but it also could be a sign that the car is bent. Unless you can prove otherwise, walk away. Also, compare the relative positions of the wheels within their arches – if one is even fractionally further forwards, backwards, inwards or outwards than the other then the car is probably bent and, in the absence of evidence to the contrary, walk away.

If your budget won't quite run to a new Mini and you're looking for one with a few thousand miles on the clock, the best advice is to shop around local dealers – preferably, your nearest Rover agent, who has a reputation to maintain – with Rover as much as among the buying public. In my experience, the local Rover dealer rarely advertises used Minis, and the best bet would be to visit the dealer and see whether he has any and, if not, to leave your address and telephone number and to let him know what sort of car you want and what sort of money you are prepared to spend. The dealer won't waste a second in telephoning you when a suitable car comes along in part-exchange, the best time being during July and August when the registration letter changes.

There are a growing number of specialist used Mini sales businesses and, if there's one near you, start your search there.

General car dealers might charge slightly less for a given Mini than a Rover main dealer because they don't have such high overheads, but they aren't answerable to Rover if they inadvertently sell you a poorly maintained and unreliable, a stolen or even a previously written-off Mini.

Of recent Minis, the stars are obviously the various limited edition cars which, by virtue of their comparative rarity, can be difficult to track down. Many end up in specialist Mini dealerships and, as a consequence, bargains are rare and you can expect to have to pay almost as much for a fairly recent limited edition as you would for a brand new car. The great benefit of buying from such a specialist is that his knowledge of the Mini should be so good that he rejects all but the very best examples – and hence, perhaps, there is a justification for the higher prices.

A dented exhaust downpipe. My best guess is that this downpipe has been rammed into a kerbstone to produce such a dent. The 'repair' (carried out on behalf of a previous owner) entailed welding the pipe to its bracket, which has resulted in the crack which by this stage extends almost right around the pipe! New downpipes, I discovered, are not 'stock' items at Rover dealers, are not available as pattern parts and – like so many Mini components – are a swine to fit. If you are not inclined to carry out such awkward repairs, it may be best to ask the vendor to have them put right before you buy the car.

I did temporarily weld the splits in the downpipe, but later decided to replace the down-pipe. To do a proper welded repair meant taking the pipe off the car and, once it *is* off, I feel it's just as well to do the job properly!

LE Minis range from simple 'paint and upholstery' specials to cars like the Open Classic with its electric sunroof. All are both latent classics and useable modern cars – you win both ways!

OLDER MINIS

Some earlier limited edition cars, say, from the early to mid-1980s, will have been driven lightly and generally cosseted in the hope that the cars would one day become extremely valuable classics which, of course, won't happen for many a year – if ever. There are as a consequence some excellent examples around. You should therefore weigh the asking price not so much on any real or imagined 'classic' value as on the actual condition of the car.

Much the same goes for the standard car. The Mini is often kept as a 'second' car, which can mean that it has received light use (a good thing) or that it has been used almost exclusively for short journeys – taking the kids to school, shopping expeditions and the like – which is not such a plus point. A predominance of short journeys will result in the engines coking up, in the oil turning a yellow ochre (an emulsion of oil and water which has condensed out onto the engine internals) and consequently higher internal wear than that of the engine of a car used for fewer but longer journeys.

Don't imagine that the standard Mini from the eighties has any monetary classic value, be guided purely by the condition of the car and keep to the 'book' prices. Only exceptionally clean cars will exceed this.

The bulk of Minis from the early eighties back might be considered classic cars but their condition dictates that they are probably more accurately described as jalopies. Priced from a couple of hundred pounds upwards (1995 values), they can provide reliable transport but their very age means that they will contain thousands of aged components – each and every one of them something of a liability – something else to go wrong. Look for a car with evidence of regular maintenance – clean ignition components and oil filter, recent drive shaft and steering rack gaiters, that sort of thing. Remember that any component which is

Lift the door trim and count the thicknesses of steel underneath. There should be two (any extras are the rotten remains of original sills) and they should be spot welded if original.

The battery box floor rots out, with the inevitable consequence that the battery eventually falls out to be dragged along under the car – not too clever! This is not an especially difficult repair to do, but you *have* to remove the fuel tank and line, plus the battery, before welding anywhere near the boot – so the job as a whole is very time-consuming.

This battery box is on an eleven-year-old Mini – the rot is worse than it looks and repair won't be far off. If not repaired, just to repeat myself, the floor will eventually give way, the battery will drop out and be dragged along the tarmac – don't fool yourself, it really will!

Even small details count. This cracked light lens will possibly result in an MOT failure (depending on the individual tester!) unless replaced – they aren't too expensive, but a lot of small items in need of replacement on a battle-weary example can add up.

covered in a layer of dust, dirt or oil has not received attention recently. The very safest such cars are those which have been garaged from new and serviced regularly by a Rover dealer. They are very much in the minority.

RESTORED MINIS

Few cars appear to make it much beyond their tenth birthday without some welded repair; many will be on their second rear subframe, which calls into question the state of the heel-board ends and sills. This is not a full guide to the appraisal of a Mini but a few general rules will help you to avoid the real lemons.

Firstly, accept that the majority of elderly Minis don't command huge values and, as a result, few people are prepared to spend enough on their restoration to do the job properly. Along with other lowish-value classics like the Minor, Beetle, A35/40 and so on, an awful lot of so-called 'restored' Minis are in fact very poorly repaired.

IMPORTANT: steer clear of any car on which you find a welded cover patch – anywhere. Patch repairs are inevitably carried out in answer to an MOT failure – a dubious measure which just allows the car to get another year's 'ticket' but which is very short-lived. Unless all rot is cut out and repair panels are welded in, the only acceptable welded repair is a butt weld. Provided that all rot has been cut out and the steel properly cleaned prior to

Look at the wing and A panel; if the line is this far out, it could be due to a poor wing replacement or – in the worst cases – a bent front end. If you cannot be sure which, steer clear of the car.

Lift the front carpets and have a peek underneath. Apart from holes and patch repairs to the floorpan, look at the wheelarch rear for filler and poor repairs, and at the toe-board for dents.

welding, surplus weld ground down (which makes the repair invisible) and the repair rust-proofed afterwards, a butt welded repair can outlast the rest of the bodywork. Sadly, most people weld on cover patches.

Secondly, check that the bodyshell isn't bent as already described. The distortion can not only be caused by collision, it can be built into a bodyshell during a poor quality restoration.

Thirdly, check the entire bodyshell for non-steel 'repairs'. Don't be surprised to find deep dents full of body filler almost anywhere on the

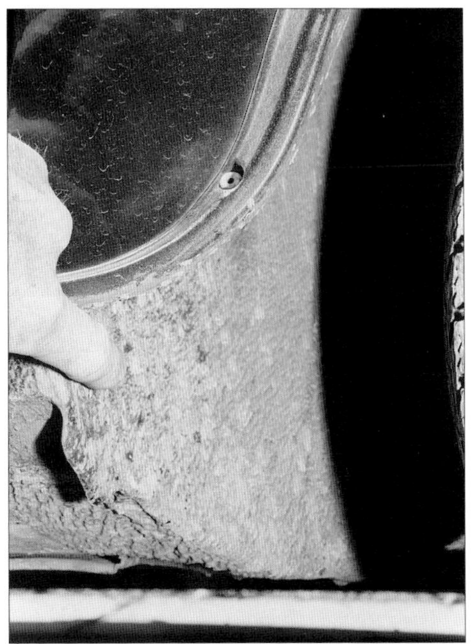

This area at the rear of the front wheelarch gets a real pounding from mud and stones etc., thrown up by the front wheels, so look for welded-on cover patches, GRP and bodyfiller 'repairs'.

shell; GRP, cardboard/wire mesh and filler bridging rotten holes. A magnet can reveal such bodges. GRP or filler in the side points to side impact, so check that the subframes are correctly aligned. The same materials in the roof or pillars suggests that the car has been rolled, in the which case, it is probably bent.

Finally, look for signs of corrugation in the flitch, rear inner wing, boot floor, floorpans and toe board – sure signs of a hefty shunt. As always, unless you feel comfortable with both the car and the vendor – walk away.

CLASSIC MINIS

You might consider your Mini a 'classic' even though it only rolled of the production line last week – that's quite up to you, and no-one can argue that your car is not a true classic. The public perception of a classic car, however, can be rather different. When does an older Mini cease to be a jalopy and become a classic? I don't know, but there is probably a crossing point somewhere during the 1970s *but,* be warned, a rotten or even a scruffy example of any year of Mini is still perceived as a jalopy.

Let's take a chance and define a classic car as

On older Minis, check for misuse of filler or GRP 'repair'. It is not unusual to find large holes bridged with a filler backed with cardboard (!) or GRP.

I made up this simple repair panel. At present, it is pop-riveted in place, ready for welding. Nowadays, I'm more inclined to tack it into position before knocking down the edge and seam welding it – a process I call 'tack it and smack it'.

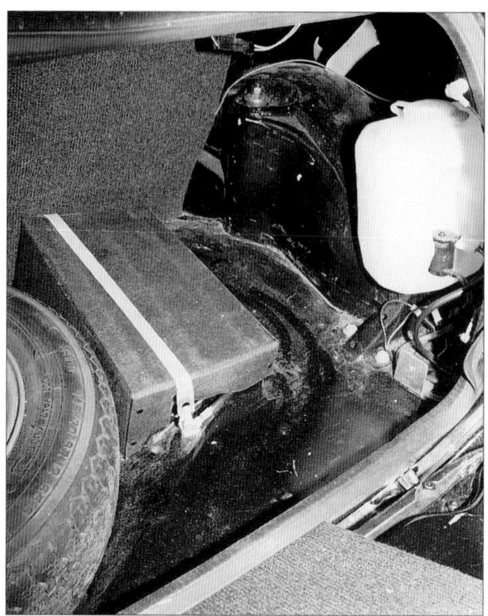

Boot Floor/Wheelarch. Heavy rear collision can corrugate the boot floor and distort the inner wheel-arch. Check the wheelarch, battery box and boot floor edges for filler or bodged welded repairs on older cars.

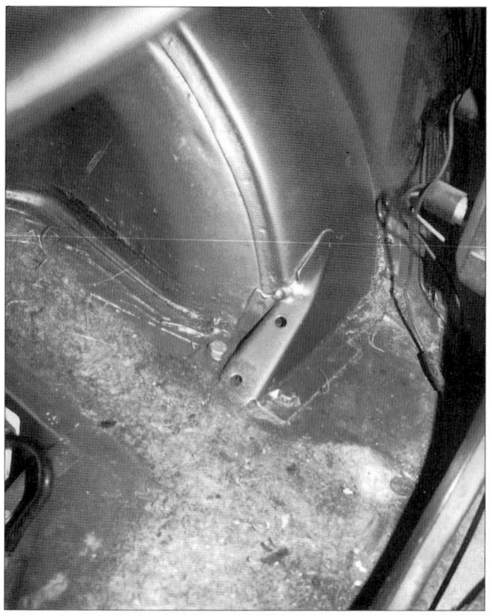

This wheelarch looks good, but closer inspection revealed filler in the lower rear wheelarch, just above the boot floor. A magnet is often the only way to find such problems.

The sources of oil leakage can be difficult to trace if the oil lands on a rotating component like the offset sphere joint or driveshaft – it will be thrown everywhere.

If you can hear a clicking noise at slow speed and full lock then a CV joint (right) is on the way out; it lives under here and any workshop manual will describe how to replace it.

one whose condition is far better than anyone has any right to expect of a car of its age. Applied to the Mini, a 1975 Clubman which is structurally sound, mechanically sorted and presentable is a classic – an example covered with rust bubbles and with a disgracefully dirty engine bay is a jalopy – and unfortunately in the majority in this neck of the woods.

Let's face facts. There are three ways in which a really good classic Mini can come onto the market. Firstly, it could have been cosseted from new, garaged and never driven when the roads were wet – in which case, its rarity value alone will command a high price. Secondly, the owner has spent many hundreds if not thousands of hours restoring the car to pristine condition – again, it will command a high price. Thirdly, the owner has spent thousands of pounds having the car professionally restored – and again the car will not come cheap. If you want a really first-class classic Mini, you'll have to pay top book. Unfortunately, this is not a reciprocal process – paying a high price is no defence against buying a jalopy!

Older cars are more liable to be bent than newer ones, simply because their age means that they have had more time on the road. Older cars also, of course, suffer bodyrot which – in the worst cases – can make the cars weak and potentially dangerous in use. The increased likelihood of an older Mini being bent or rotten means that, even though the value may be far less than that of a more recent car, you have to be even more scrupulous when checking it out. If in doubt, summon professional help.

With the rare exception of a car which has been 'mothballed' from new because of the original owner's half-baked notion that it will as a result in a few years' time become a fabulously valuable classic, expect all older Minis to have received some degree of welded bodywork repair. The art of assessing monocoque classic cars is very much the art of assessing bodywork repair standards.

The most easily checked panels are *the external body panels* – look for rivelling, test for filler and GRP and look for signs of localised repair which indicate that the car has been tarted-up for sale – *the flitch panels inside the engine bay* – rivelling indicates that the car has been in a shunt – *the toeboard* – deep dents here could be the only visible evidence of a bent car – *the heelboard and side stowage cubbies* – hot rot spots – and *the boot interior* – rivelling means collision and rot means expensive repairs are needed.

Be sure to take in the wider view, by which I mean standing back and looking at the whole car to see whether the front end is askew (a common result when a front end shunt car is 'repaired'), whether the door gaps are even both sides of the car, whether (with both doors open) the sills lie in the same plane. That sort of thing.

If you don't mind getting dirty, check out the rear subframe. Most aged Minis will be on their second or third subframe and, if you see welded repairs, forget it. Also check out the sills and the floorpan edges – 'upside-down' welding indicates poor repair.

BOGUS CLASSICS

It is a sad fact that the prices realised by the more desirable Minis during the 'silly money' days of the late 1980s were so high that some unscrupulous types found it profitable to construct counterfeit cars – fake Mini Coopers. There are several potential 'give-aways' to a fake Cooper, and they are all well known to Cooper fans but, because they *are* well-known, counterfeiters are also aware of them and can accommodate the necessary alterations. If you want a Cooper then get expert help; there are several exhaustive 'originality' or 'authenticity' guide books which might help spot a forgery (although remember that counterfeiters can also consult the books), and there is no substitute for bringing in a Cooper expert to check out cars for you. Contact the Mini clubs and registers to see whether they have a member in

Modified Bodywork Minis. Tread carefully – a lot are crude bodges. Example; de-seaming involves grinding away a short length of seam, continuous welding the joint, then grinding away the next length. Some folk smash the old seam inwards with a lump hammer, and smooth it off with oodles of bodyfiller.

your vicinity. Best of all (if you can afford it), buy a well-known example, and make doubly sure it is not a 'ringer'.

WHAT TO PAY – CLASSIC MINIS

Place little faith in published classic car value guides other than those which are Mini-specific and preferably published by an owners' club. A classic Mini has three values: the vendor's asking price, the price you are prepared to pay and the price someone else is prepared to pay. The important one is the price you are prepared or able to pay.

When looking for a car, I firstly set myself a strict budget limit. If I cannot find the car I want in the condition I want and within my budget then I simply go without – I still don't own an E-Type Jaguar, an MG TF or a Ford GT40! If I'm looking for a restoration project car, that's another matter. I assess cars according to how much they will cost to restore, plus the asking price and, if the total exceeds my budget, I again go without.

The values of Mini Coopers, Mokes and limited edition cars are fairly well established, and any Mini club worthy of the name should be able to advise on current market values. With other Minis, the only valuation of any real worth is what a particular example is worth to you. We could list current prices in this book, but they would probably simply be misleading.

MODIFIED MINIS

Few cars which have been 'hotted-up' are worth anything like as much as they have cost their owners. Unless the performance components and work carried out are of the highest quality, a modified Mini can not only be worth less than one in good original condition, but also be more difficult to sell. It's a buyer's market, so take your time.

When assessing modified cars, ignore the flash and concentrate on the basics – bodyrot, bodyshell distortion – because many amateur customisers don't bother frittering money on boring things like rotting sills, but spend their entire budget on shiny goodies and go-faster bits. Minis with performance conversion work should be checked out professionally, because there's so much at stake (like your life!).

CUSTOM MINIS

The very, very worst bodges I have ever heard about or seen on any car have been the work of amateur 'customisers', and the really aggravating thing is that, once a rotten bodyshell has been plastered with many pounds of bodyfiller and painted, it can be difficult for the non-expert to tell the death-trap from the delectable. I once bought a Morris Minor which had been 'customised' (expecting the worst but having those expectations exceeded), and found that a stiffening swage line on the quarter panel had been ground away and replaced by corrugated cardboard on the inside, plastered with bodyfiller on the outside.

To achieve a 'smooth' look, the same customiser had smashed a convex line inwards and again covered up the evidence with filler, and had resorted yet again to filler to hide advanced rot from around the rear wheelarch.

If I wanted a custom Mini (which I don't) then I'd build it myself. I would not contemplate buying a car which – however good it looked – could be a coming together of a jalopy and several jumbo-sized tins of bodyfiller. If you are determined to buy one, then at the very least insist on seeing photographic evidence that the work was carried out properly and get a motor engineer's report on the thing before buying it.

There are good custom cars out there – it's sorting the roadworthy (the minority) from the wreck that's the problem.

LIMITED EDITION MINIS

There have to date been 26 releases of Limited Edition Minis, comprising 31 models ranging from the 1975 Mini 1000 Special right up to the 1995 Mini Sidewalk. A grand total of 50,500 LE Minis (spanning nearly two decades) means that there is a usually a reasonable choice of Limited Edition Minis, ranging from bedraggled to brand-new. Obviously the older the car, the greater the chance of finding collision damage evidence or bodyrot. More recent Limited Edition Minis provide increasingly reliable motoring, but with the exclusivity of driving an LE car, and are highly recommended.

Really good, low mileage LE Minis are desirable classics; average LE Minis are more desirable than the standard car, but do remember that a LE Mini which is rotten or which has uncorrected or poorly corrected crash damage is a jalopy.

Check the wheels of LE Minis for damage, including scuffing; these are not cheap!

LE Minis made before and during the 1980s were widely assumed to be so-called 'future classics' and, because *all* classic cars appeared to be fetching silly prices during the heady days of the late 1980s (and because this trend was expected to continue ad infinitum) people were prepared to 'invest' considerable sums tarting-up damaged LE Minis as 'investment cars' – so be on your guard. Also, LE Minis with exceptionally low mileages do fetch reasonable money, so you have to check for any evidence of 'clocking' – winding back the miles. Signs include mis-aligned digits on the mileometer, but also signs of general wear in the interior which don't match the car's claimed mileage. If possible, ask to see past MOT certificates, which should all show a slowly rising mileage. A full service history is a definite plus point. While on the subject of very low mileage Minis, don't lose sight of the fact that engines can age much more rapidly in a car used for short journeys, and a 50,000 miler can in this respect turn out to be a better prospect than a car with a tenth of that mileage.

In addition to the checks recommended earlier in this chapter, add the following for all Limited Edition Minis.

1. Signs of forced entry; locks, areas around locks, replacement steering lock, scratches around radio – especially any Mini with a Cooper badge which is attractive to joyriders.
2. Alloy wheels. Scuffing – car kerbed – these wheels might prove expensive to replace.
3. Exclusive interior trim – might prove very expensive to replace if in poor condition.
4. Mileage. With low mileage cars, look at the oil on the dipstick (it should be clear, indicating regular oil changes), and look in the rocker box cover for signs of yellow emulsion (water condensation mixed with oil as a result of too many short journeys – engine wear might be high, irrespective of miles travelled). Check indicated mileage against condition of interior trim, and watch for renewed pedal rubbers which have replaced worn-out originals.
5. Autodata check for stolen/recovered or crash write-off advisable.
6. Garage forecourt aerosol tart-up. I've seen a used-car dealer quite openly spray paint from an aerosol can over an area with surface rusting. Run your finger tips over the paint at the scuttle ends, all paintwork at the front of the car (stone chip damage) and around the quarter panel and rear quarters. Synthetic paints don't shrink, and any overspray can be felt.

WHAT'S AVAILABLE: LIMITED EDITION MINIS

1975. *Mini 1000 Special.* 3,000 manufactured, original price £1,406. Coming up to 20 years old at the time of writing, launched when the classic car movement was in its infancy and won't have been cosseted as a 'future classic' like later specials, so few will have survived in good condition. Look for standards of bodywork repair/restoration, and be on your guard against nice-looking but bodged examples.

1979. *Mini 20, 1,100cc Special.* Original price £3,300. Metallic paint, upgraded interior, alloys. An old car, so check for repair standards. 5,000 made, but not too many survivors – a good one is exclusive. A very nice car.

1983. *Mini Sprite.* 2,500 manufactured, original price £3,334. Yellow/Red with alloys, side decals and a nice interior, good original examples rare today. Most will have received some 'restoration', so watch out for bodged cars.

1984. *Mini 25 'Silver Jubilee'.* Original price £3,865. Distinctive but, with 5,000 made and just 11 years old, not yet a rarity (these cars were more coveted than and did tend to be better looked-after than earlier specials). 998cc engine, front discs, recliners with velour trim. Look for FSH or evidence of regular servicing. A good one is well worth having.

1985-7. *The 'London Collection'.* Up-market luxury Ritz, Chelsea, Piccadilly and Park Lane.

1985. *Ritz.* Silver leaf. 3,725 made; original price £3,798. Quite a few survivors; so try to find a well-maintained example – neglected ten-year-old cars don't cost much to buy but can cost serious money to keep in roadworthy condition.

1985. *Chelsea.* Targa red with Osprey grey cloth interior. 1,500 made; original price £3,898. Distinctive, fairly rare and desirable.

1986. *Piccadilly.* Gold, 2,500 made; original price £3,928. Quite a few still available, so shop around.

1987. *Park Lane.* Black with velour trim. 1,500 made; original price £4,193. Up-market, desirable LE Mini.

1987. *Advantage.* Tennis theme – the 1st 'designer' Mini. Diamond White with logos, jade trim. 2,500 made; original price £4,286. Desirable – some nice examples to be found but watch out for bodged bodywork repairs. Remember that rust staining stands out like a sore thumb on white cars; staining under just one body seam cover probably indicates crash damage repair – no staining at all could be a good sign, but check for aerosol can tart-up over-spray.

1988. *Red Hot/Jet Black.* Retro/designer theme. Striking colour schemes, 2,000 production run; original price £4,382 – popular then and now.

1988. *Designer* – the name says it all! Black or Diamond White. Interior by Mary Quant. 2,000 made; original price £4,654. White cars – see Mini Advantage.

1989. *Rose/Sky*. Tasteful 60s retro; very bright and cheerful Mini. Maybe overlooked to date, but will probably be popular in years to come. 1,000 made; original price £4,695. At the time of writing, fairly recent cars which should not yet have suffered much from rusting, so if you find rust or bodyfiller, suspect collision damage as the cause. See comments re. white cars – Mini Advantage. Rare and recommended.

1989. *Flame/Racing*. Red/BRG. Celebrating 30 years of motorsport. 2,000 made; original price £4,795. Next, the return of the Cooper.

Racing, Flame, Rose and Sky. All nice, but there's something about the Rose and Sky which sets them apart from other Limited Edition cars – bright, breezy and unpretentious – exactly what a Mini ought to be.

1989. *Mini Thirty*. Way up-market; leather, alloys etc. 3,000 made (2,000 pearlescent Cherry Red, 1,000 Black); original price £5,599, many still on road, some with bodywork deterioration. A good one is a very nice car, but many on the general used-car market seem over-priced – check out Mini specialists.

1990. *Flame/Racing/Checkmate*. Flame and Racing back by popular demand! Another 2,500; original price £5,455.

1990. *Studio 2*. Designer Mini in Steel Grey. 2,000 made; original price £5,375. Pretty exclusive and recent enough to offer a choice of good original examples.

1990. *Cooper*. 1,000 made with signed 'Cooper' stripes and body-colour wheelarches; original price £6,995 – v. exclusive *if* you can A) find, and B) afford one.

1991. *Neon*. 'Nordic' Blue. Loads of chrome. 1,500 made; original price £5,570. General car dealers over-optimistic in pricing. Nice special.

Sporting rather more chrome than its contemporaries, the Neon (top) in Caribbean Blue was a mixture of 1960s and 1990s style; just 1,500 produced, so opportunities to buy one now will be few and far between.

A racing-certainty to become a classic in more than name, the Mini British Open Classic (above) is a joy to drive on hot summer days when the occupants of tin-tops are sweltering!

1991. *LAMM Cabriolet.* Pearl Cherry, wide alloys. Only 75 made; original price £12,250. Needless to say, opportunities to buy will probably prove as rare as hen's teeth, and you'll have to be prepared to out-bid several other hopefuls if you want one!

1992. *British Open Classic.* BRG with a half-leather interior. Just 1,000 made and sold at a 'classic' £7,195! Full-length electric sunroof etc. accounted for the high price. 1.3 litre engine and cat, but good old SU carb supplying the fuel. In my opinion, strangely and massively under-valued in published price guides, and an excellent car to own in its own right – let alone as a latent desirable classic. Buy the best you can find, then, on the hottest day of the year, set to with anti-rust treatments – keep a British Open Classic in good order and one day you'll find that it's one of the most desirable of all the LE Minis.

1992. *Italian Job.* 1,750 made; Red/White or Blue and some BRG; original price £5,995. Largely cosmetic but hugely evocative and highly sought-after because of it.

1993. *Rio.* Unashamedly a 'fashion' Mini. Only 750 made; original price £5,495. Paintwork and interior upgraded. Good future prospect if you want an exclusive recent Mini.

1993. *Tahiti.* Only 500 made; original price £5,795. Another fashion Mini, but none the worse for that. A good one to buy and cherish for the future.

My favourite LE Mini – and not just because there's one on my drive (though it helps!). Park this car alongside a load of modern stuff, and people will remark how nice it looks; the reason why it catches their eye is the abundance of chrome.

1994. ***Mini 35 SE.*** 1,000 made in Red, White or Blue; original price £5,695. A bit extra-special and in my opinion under-valued in published guides. If you don't believe me, try and find a really nice one at published value guide prices! Interestingly, the Mini 35 for Japan was based upon the Mayfair, with leather seats.

With a production run of just 500, the Mini Tahiti will never be a common sight and a bit special for it.

1994. ***Mini Cooper Monte Carlo LE.*** 200 made; original price £7,995. We all want one! These cars tend to be cosseted, but some will have been given a serious thrashing. Be wary of any at less than top book – if, that is, you can find one!

1995. ***Mini Sidewalk.*** 1,000 made; price £5,895. Designer plus! Very distinctive Tartan interior and unmistakable livery make this a worthy addition to the LE Mini lineage.

1995. ***Mini Cooper S.*** Price £9.975. Not strictly speaking a Rover Limited Edition Mini, but a fully Rover-approved after-market conversion by The Master himself. A brand new Rover Mini Cooper is ordered by John Cooper Garages on behalf of and registered in the name of the customer, breathed upon and made plusher and more sure-footed. The lucky customer gets 80bhp, 86 lbs/ft of torque, and a 0-60mph time of 9.86 seconds.

If you are fortunate enough to own one of these gorgeous cars – DON'T BEND IT or you'll be answerable to me!

Just 200 Mini Cooper Monte Carlo Limited Edition were made; some will be mothballed and hoarded as 'investments'; others will have been driven with gusto. If you want one then you'll quickly discover that this is a seller's market, and ever likely to remain so. Grey painted alloy wheels with hub badges, 165 section tyres.

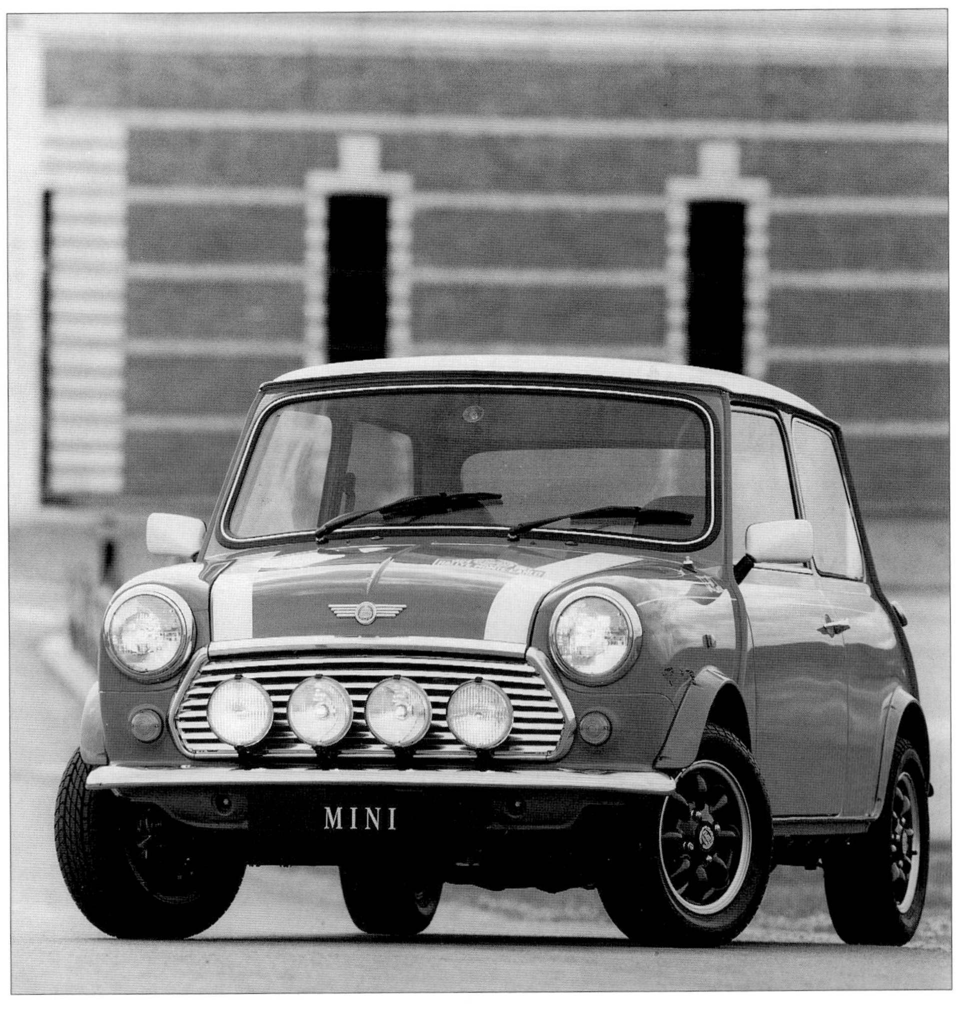

Official cabriolets (top) look so much better than after-market conversions – the Mini Cabriolet. is a real beaut. The hood was developed by Tickford and the car based upon the Cooper 1.3i (63 PS) powertrain.

'Sidewalk' (above) is very much a North American term, and why a Mini Limited Edition with tartan interior should be so named is a mystery to this author. Not a gripe, this is a lovely car.

While major Japanese car makers have been setting up manufacturing plants here in the UK., Rover has been quietly exporting Minis in some quantities (with a 12,000 peak in 1990) to seemingly insatiable Japanese Mini fanatics. Far be it for me to suggest that the Japanese people might have better taste in cars than Europeans! All cars have air conditioning.

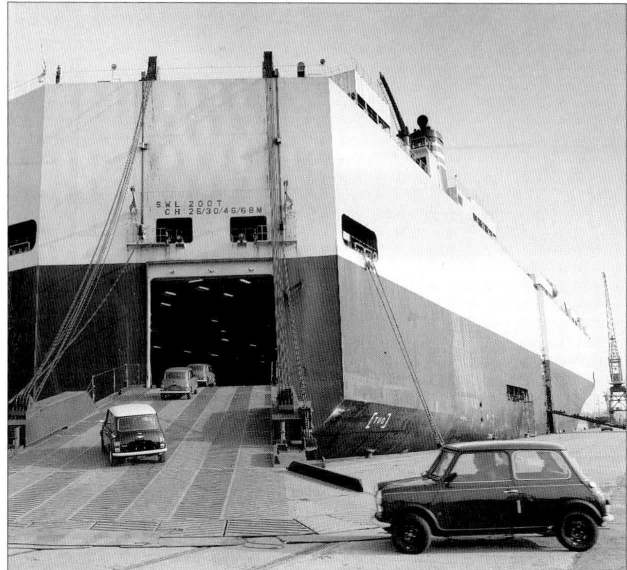

Just LOOK at those seats – makes you want to buy a Sidewalk just to sink into them!

CHAPTER TWO

Survival for (and in) your MINI

The Mini is renowned for its reliability but, if regular maintenance is neglected, even the Mini quickly becomes unreliable, thirsty, often difficult to start in the morning and prone to on-road breakdowns. Worse, a lack of maintenance quickens the demise of many mechanical components, and can lead to expensive repairs being needed.

Basic maintenance of the Mini is generally straightforward and within the capabilities of any able-bodied person. You don't require masses of special tools, either, in order to keep your Mini in tip-top roadworthy condition. One item which is really essential is a good workshop manual; be sure to obtain one which includes the appropriate year and model. A good workshop manual should not only include all the service data for your own Mini but will also go into greater detail in explaining how various jobs are tackled than is possible in a 'glove box' book like this.

Maintenance breaks down into three specific areas; the most frequent (weekly) maintenance consists mainly of a series of checks that the various fluid levels are correct, tyres are undamaged and properly inflated – and so on. No tools other than a good jack and axle stands, tyre pressure gauge and a foot pump are required. These checks can often reveal developing faults which, if left to their own devices, will eventually mature into on-road – sometimes terminal – breakdowns. The second level of maintenance – servicing – encompasses basic checks and supplements them with the routine replacement of components such as spark plugs and consumables such as engine oil. A small toolkit is required.

The third level of maintenance again includes the checks and work previously mentioned, in addition to which other components come in for periodic replacement, and the ignition timing, valve clearances and carburation are checked. In order to undertake this work,

As a general rule, the earlier the car, the easier the maintenance. If you think space is at a premium in the standard Mini engine bay, then get a load of the ERA Turbo! There's just about room in the top offside rear to squeeze in a spare fuse holder or maybe a spare spark plug.

If you can beg the use of an inspection pit then do so, because it turns many jobs from dirty and incredibly unpleasant to merely dirty and unpleasant.

This is how most people have to work on their cars. The minimum requirement for working on a car is a level, firm surface. Concrete is best; on tarmac and especially in hot weather, place a board under the jack to stop it sinking into the surface.

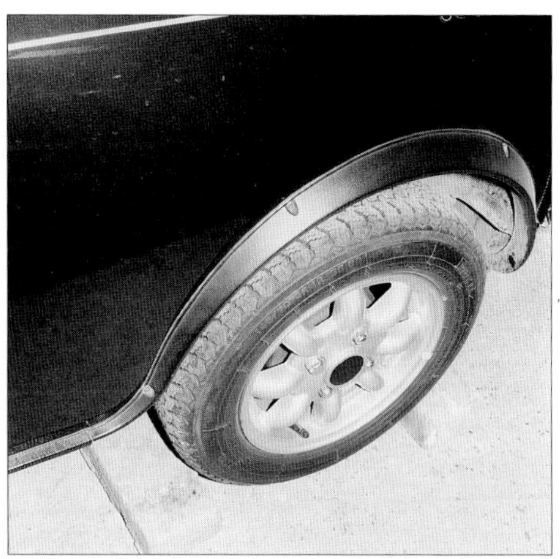

Wheel chocked. You can buy wheel chocks, but in practice most people seem to opt to use house-bricks or similar. For a roadside wheel change, use whatever is to hand – anything is better than nothing!

you'll need firstly to assemble a fairly comprehensive toolkit but, because the costs of the tools required can be less than the cost of having the work carried out professionally – the outlay is in effect immediately recouped.

Ideally, every driver should be well enough acquainted with his or her car to be able to undertake the first and second levels of maintenance. By carrying out this work, you learn much about the workings of the car and, as a result, you are more likely to be able to sort out problems such as breakdowns for yourself. The alternative is to trust to the professionals and to have the car serviced at the prescribed times – the problem with which is that the most basic and ideally frequently-needed checks are only carried out at far greater intervals.

SAFETY

The little Mini is in fact a surprisingly heavy car, quite capable of causing you serious injury if it were to fall on to any part of your body. For this reason, you should never work under the car unless it is supported by sturdy axle stands – the sole exception being roadside wheel changes. Remember that a jack is a lifting device and that it is not intended actually to support weight for any length of time. Axle stands don't cost a lot and are more versatile than drive-on ramps because they allow you to remove wheels from the raised car (for brake maintenance), which ramps obviously do not permit.

The small scissors or wind-up jack which you carry in the car is intended only for roadside wheel changes – for workshop use, buy a 2 ton bottle jack or preferably a small trolley jack, both of which are more stable and hence safer. Before you raise the car, place chocks both fore and aft of the two wheels which are to remain on the ground – you don't want the car to roll off the jack or axle stands!

To raise the front of the car, place a fairly thick piece of softwood padding on top of the jack, and lift the car by the sump. To raise the rear of the car, again use padding, but place the jack under the subframe. To raise one side of the car, use the jacking point or – if this is suspect or you are using a trolley jack, locate it under the central crossmember – again, with wood packing. Still on the subject of safety, remember that you will be dealing with certain

When tightening wheelnuts, don't overdo it! Firm arm pressure is quite sufficient – if you ever want to get the nuts back off, that is! Check the wheelnuts' tightness after a few miles.

potentially hazardous substances and forces. Brake fluid – modern silicone types excepted – is capable of damaging paintwork and, more importantly, your skin. It is also highly flammable, as is petrol and most especially petrol vapour, so keep both away from any possible source of combustion. Don't breathe in petrol fumes – which means never sucking on a pipe to siphon fuel! Old engine oil can cause skin problems, so wear disposable plastic gloves to keep this away from your skin.

Electricity can not only give you an electric shock (a real 'belt' if it involves the high tension – 25,000 volts – circuitry) but can also be the cause of fires. A tiny electric spark is sufficient to ignite combustible vapours; a short circuit can heat wire to the point that its

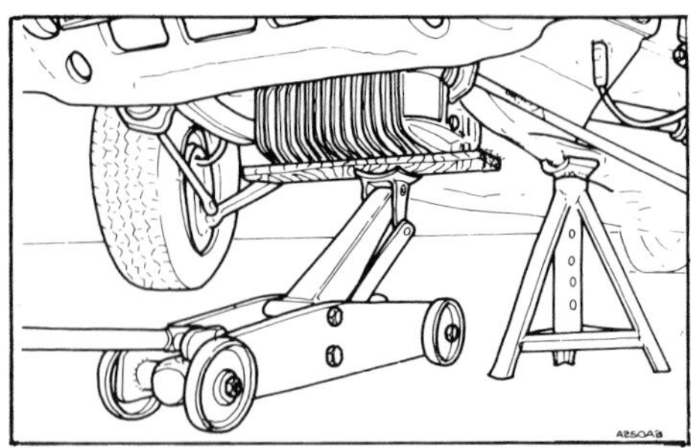

The usual prescribed method of raising the front end of a Mini – if you do this, then use thick softwood to protect the sump. The alternative is to raise the car by the subframe, under the lower suspension arm end – again, using wood packing. *(All diagrams courtesy Autodata)*

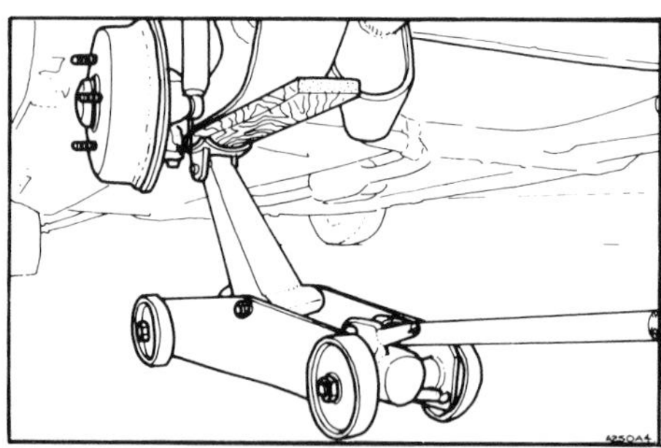

Raising the rear of the car. If your car has a steering lock, then engage it before chocking the front wheels.

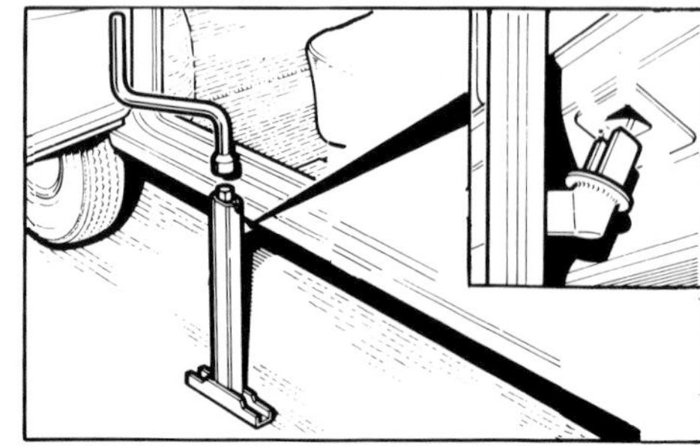

Using the jack to raise one side of the car. This really is suitable only for roadside wheel changes – use a bottle or trolley jack in the workshop.

To use the standard jack, the door has to be open; as the side rises, it will swing back – so get ready to catch it. By way of a safety measure, try putting the wheel underneath the sill while the car is raised – if it does topple from the jack, it will hopefully damage the wheel rather than your person – the lesser of two evils!

Car raised on axle stand. Engage the steering lock, chock the front wheels, raise the car and support it on axle stands before working on it.

insulation firstly melts then catches fire – ALWAYS disconnect the battery (earth terminal first) before working on the car's electrics.

Finally, you've only got two of them, they're easily damaged and transplants are not available – wear eye protection at all times.

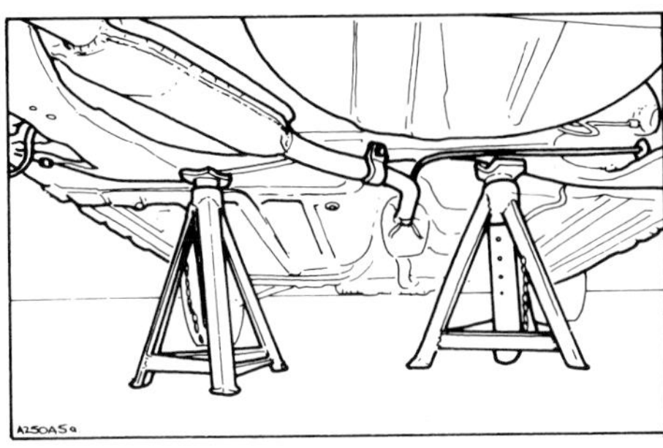

Don't work under a car until you've got it firmly supported on axle stands as shown.

MAINTENANCE – WEEKLY CHECKS

1. Engine oil. 2. Engine coolant. 3. Brake/clutch fluid. 4. Tyre condition and inflation. 5. Lights, electrics and washer bottle.

1. Engine oil

The engine should not have run for some time. Pull the dipstick out, wipe the end then replace it, taking care not to get dirt on it in the process. Remove it again and immediately hold it horizontally. The oil level should be between the two marks on the dipstick, which indicate the maximum and minimum acceptable levels. If the level is a little low or towards the lower mark on the dipstick, top it up by pouring a small amount of fresh engine oil into the filler hole, atop the rocker box cover. Leave it for a couple of minutes to drain down into the sump, then re-check and top up further if necessary. Don't over-fill the engine, because too much oil is nearly as bad as too little.

If the oil level is substantially down, then oil is being lost externally or burnt internally. Look for signs of external leakage and, if none is found, you have to assume that the loss is internal and caused by the oil being burnt. This means that it is entering the combustion chamber(s), either past the piston rings (an engine rebuild may be needed soon), past the valve

Absolute beginner's homework. If you don't know what the various components to be found under the bonnet are called, study this drawing. Refer back to it if necessary. The internal combustion engine is annoyingly bitty, but you've done harder things ...

stems in the cylinder head, indicating a need for a cylinder head overhaul or – possibly – crankcase pressure is forcing oil through the breather system into the carb – all serious, all requiring immediate attention. If you run the

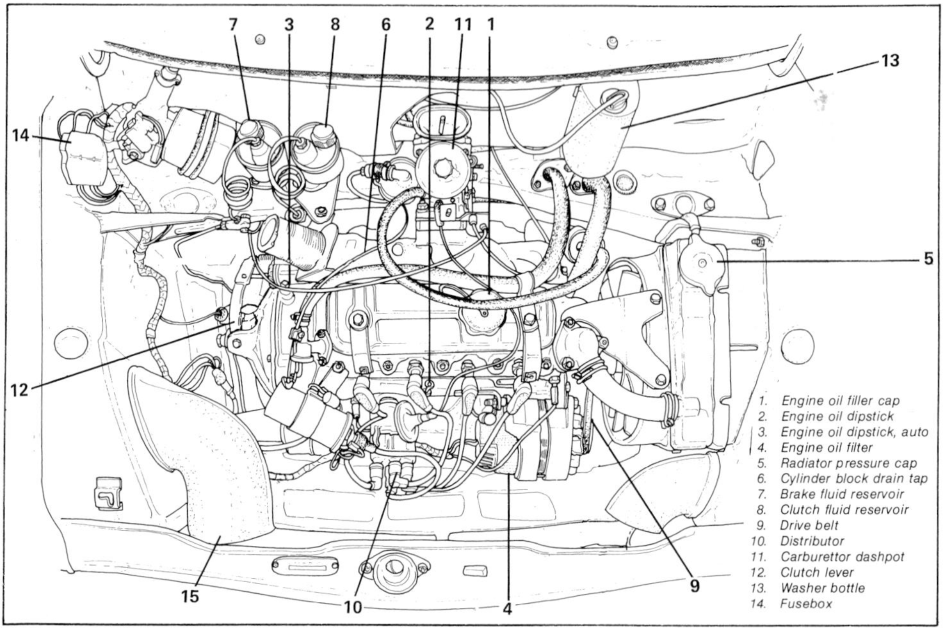

1. Engine oil filler cap
2. Engine oil dipstick
3. Engine oil dipstick, auto
4. Engine oil filter
5. Radiator pressure cap
6. Cylinder block drain tap
7. Brake fluid reservoir
8. Clutch fluid reservoir
9. Drive belt
10. Distributor
11. Carburettor dashpot
12. Clutch lever
13. Washer bottle
14. Fusebox

Checking oil level. Oil not only lubricates the engine (as if that's not important enough by itself) but also cleans it and helps to cool it. You cannot check the oil level too frequently. The oil need not be bang on the 'Max' mark, but should be close to it.

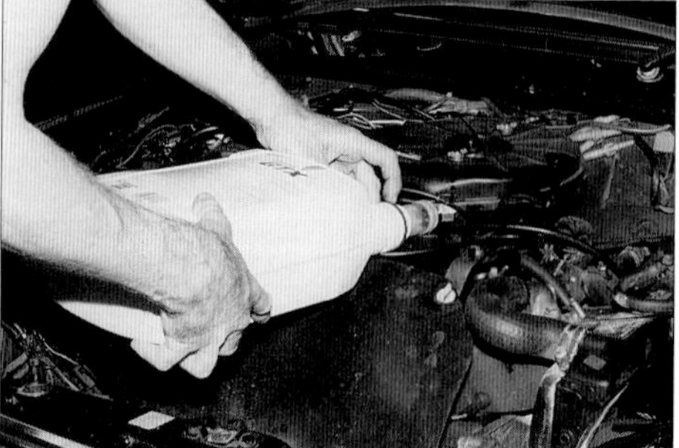

Topping up engine oil. Note how the container is held; this stops the oil suddenly surging out and missing the filler. Don't pour in much more than a pint at a time, leave this to drain down to the sump, and re-check the level.

engine with low oil, damage to the engine internals can be swift and severe. See Chapter Four for more details.

2. Engine coolant

Engine coolant becomes very hot when the engine is run – 160 degrees is not an untypical temperature. This heat causes the liquid plus the small amount of air in the system to expand, so pressurising it. If you remove the radiator cap when the coolant is thus pressurised, the result will be a gush of scalding coolant – so don't do it! Unless the engine is stone cold, check that there is no pressure in the engine coolant by squeezing the top hose. If no pressure can be felt, remove the radiator cap – carefully.

If the coolant level is low, top it up, noting how much goes in and using a mixture of water and anti-freeze in the following proportions. For envisaged temperatures down to -13 degrees Celsius 25% antifreeze, -19 degrees 33% antifreeze and -36 degrees 50% antifreeze. If you don't know what concentration of antifreeze is in your radiator, your nearest garage can measure it for you and bring it up to strength or – alternatively – low cost hydrometers calibrated for this purpose can be acquired at most motor accessory shops. If coolant is being lost in any great quantity, look for signs of external leakage, especially on the radiator and its fins, and at the ends of hoses – in both cases, leakage might be apparent as staining left by the antifreeze. Also, try running the engine up to temperature and checking visually for leakage, or pressurise the system using one of the small hand pumps available from most motor factors. If no external loss can be found then the loss is probably internal and due to a blown cylinder head gasket (which must be replaced) or a cracked cylinder head or

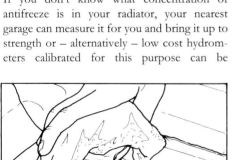

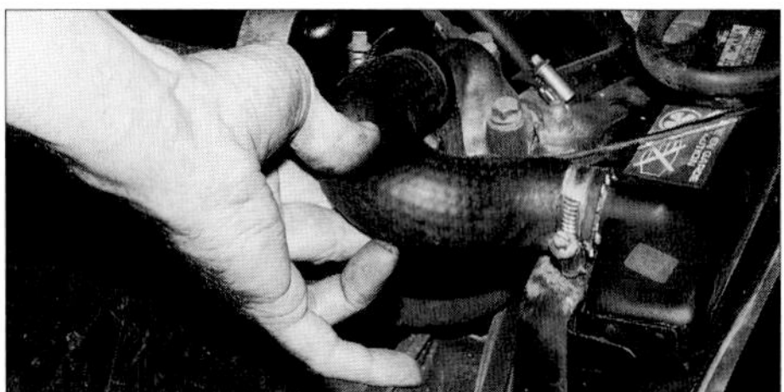

Squeezing the top hose. I once (many years ago!) collected a face full of scalding engine coolant after removing the radiator cap without firstly checking that the pressure had subsided. If you feel pressure in the top hose, kick you heels until it's gone before removing the cap.

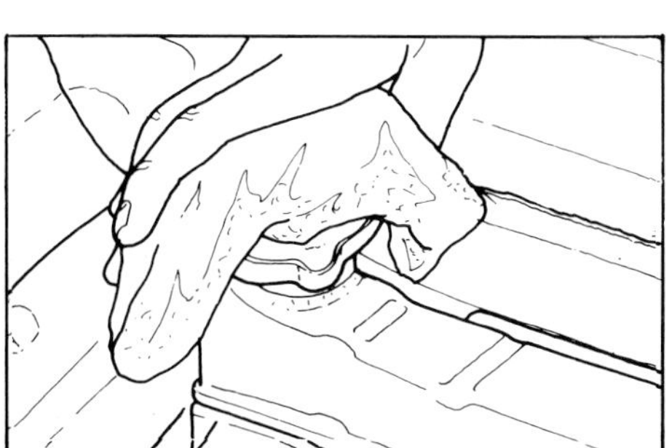

A good precaution when removing the radiator cap is to hold it using cloth as shown here. Keep pressing down as you turn the cap and, if you fell pressure or you hear coolant escaping, fasten the cap and leave the engine to cool further.

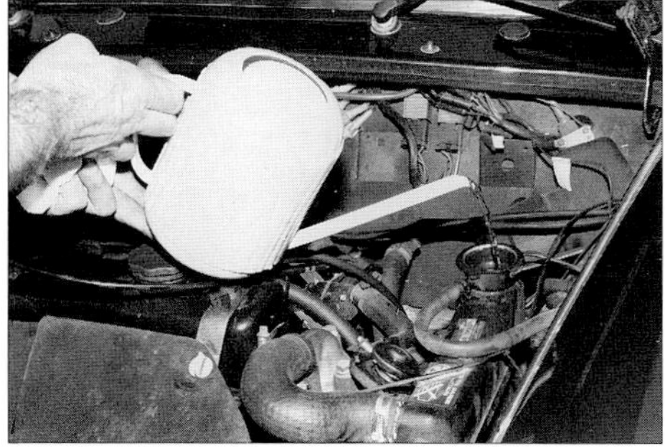

Topping up radiator. Pre-mix water and antifreeze according to envisaged temperatures. If the level is down much, it will pay to establish the cause of the leakage before using the car for journeys of more than a few miles' duration.

block – expensive. Coolant lost internally is often apparent as a large cloud of water vapour issuing from the exhaust when the engine is started after being idle for several hours – water vapour disappears, whereas smoke drifts away.

3. Brake/clutch fluid

The brake and clutch fluid reservoirs are situated on the rear bulkhead of the engine compartment. As stated in the preamble, ordinary hydraulic fluid strips paint and is flammable; in addition it is hydroscopic (able to absorb water – which can lead to brake failure in some instances). For these reasons, when you next come to change (or have changed) the fluid, you are strongly advised to re-fill the system with modern silicone-based fluid. Another advantage with silicon hydraulic fluids is that it won't – unlike ordinary fluids – need changing ever three years!

Remove the tops of the reservoirs and check the levels. If either is slightly down, top it up but keep an eye on it in case this is the start of

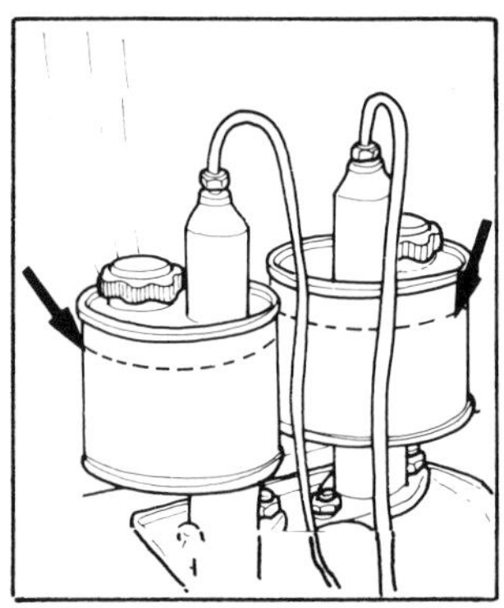

Left: brake master cylinder (the larger of the two). Right: the clutch master cylinder. Fail to maintain hydraulic fluid levels and you could end up with no brakes, no clutch – either way, it's No Go. If the level in either master cylinder does drop, it is best not to use the car until the fault has been rectified.

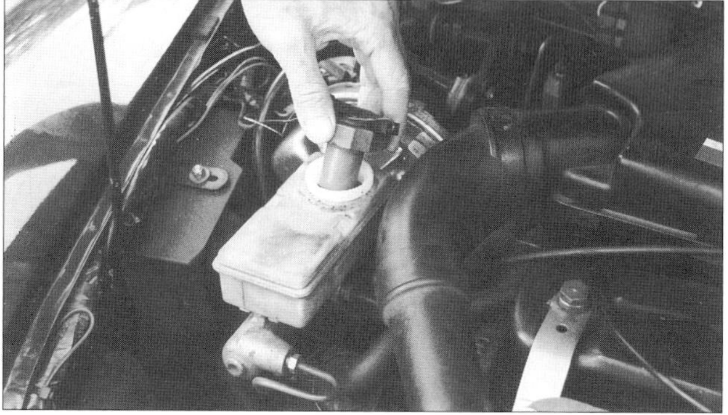

Brake master cylinder – late car with servo (above). Most hydraulic fluids make effective paint strippers; place a cloth around the master cylinder to catch any spillage. When you come to renew the fluid, it is worth considering using silicone fluid – it doesn't strip paint, doesn't have to be renewed, and doesn't absorb water.

Clutch master cylinder. Remove the air filter and you'll find it much easier to pour fluid into the clutch master cylinder without spilling most of it. Bear in mind that hydraulic fluids are highly combustible: mop up any spillage before running the engine!

a major leak. If your hands aren't steady and you are worried about splashing fluid, place a cloth around the reservoirs. If the level in either reservoir has dropped substantially (by ¼ in. or more) since the last check, it is advisable to find and rectify the leak before using the car on the road.

4. Tyre condition and pressure

Chock the two wheels which are to remain on the ground, raise one end or side of the car and support it on axle stands. Examine the tyres for cuts, abrasions, bulges and, if any are found, replace the wheel concerned with the spare and have the problem attended to. Check the tyre tread for wear – the legal tread depth can be subject to change, so find out the current legal requirements (any tyre centre or garage should be able to tell you this) and, if the tread depth is questionable, have the tyre checked out at any quick-fit centre or garage.

If the wear is uneven, this is a symptom of some other problem which needs to be addressed. If wear is concentrated at the centre of the pattern, the tyres have been over-

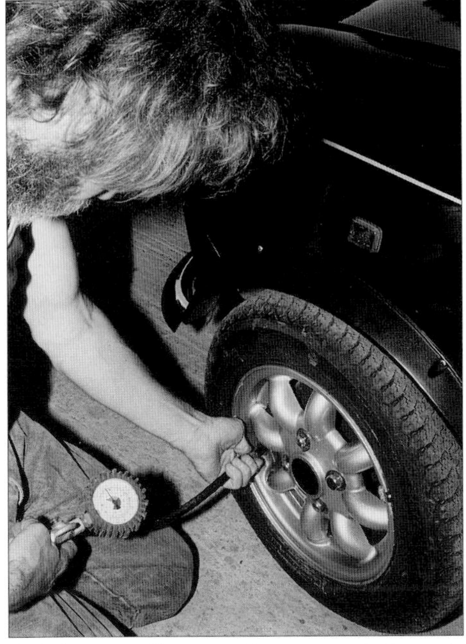

Inflating tyres. I have a small compressor in the workshop – I'm lucky. A foot pump will do the job and those small electric compressors are a good alternative.

Gauge in use. A small tyre pressure gauge like this is quite accurate enough. Keep it clean and dry, though, or you'll get false readings. Don't forget to replace the dust cap afterwards.

Checking the spare. Your spare tyre is useless if it's flat – check it regularly – preferably weekly.

inflated: if wear is greatest at the edges, under-inflated. If wear is concentrated on one side of the pattern, the causes and consequences vary greatly between front and rear wheels. If front wheels have all the wear on one side of the tread, the tracking is most probably out of alignment – have this attended to professionally – it only costs a few pounds. If a rear tyre has all the wear concentrated on one side of the tread, this could be due to simple mis-alignment of the radius arm (consult a workshop manual or have it rectified professionally) or it could indicate wear in the radius arm/pivot shaft bearings (same as above) or – in the worst cases – it could indicate serious problems including uncorrected collision damage causing mis-alignment of the rear subframe. In any event, have it checked out professionally unless you really know what you're doing.

Lower the car to the ground and check the tyre pressures.

Tyre wear patterns can reveal a host of maladies, including over and under-inflation, out of kilter tracking or more serious fundamental problems with wheel alignment.

5. Lights and Electrics

Operate the lights, stop lamps and indicators while an observer checks that they are all functioning correctly. Check that the windscreen wipers and washer pump function. (MOT failure point? You bet.) Check the level of the washer bottle and top up if necessary.

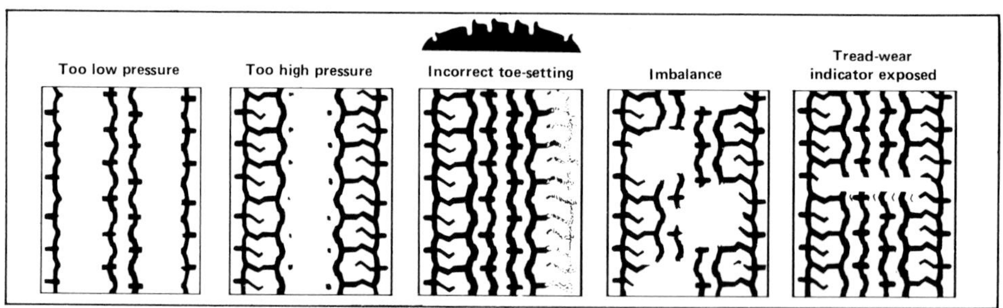

Battery electrolyte level. Check this periodically. If the level falls, the chances are that your generator is over-charging, so have that checked before it boils all the electrolyte off.

Checking battery with multi-meter. A meter such as this can reveal the state of the battery, and is potentially much less messy than using a hydrometer. Meters like this aren't especially cheap, but well worth having. You can also check the charging rate.

SERVICE – 3 MONTHLY OR EVERY 3,000 MILES (WHICHEVER COMES SOONER)

Toolkit – in addition to maintenance tools. Set of imperial spanners sizes $\frac{1}{4}$ in. to $\frac{15}{16}$ in. – a socket set in the same sizes is very useful. Spark plug box spanner (or socket if you buy a socket set). One small adjustable spanner. Selection of straight blade and Philips head screwdrivers. Pliers. Side cutters. Wire brush. Emery cloth. Grease gun and multi-purpose, high temperature lithium-based grease. Brake adjusting spanner. Feeler gauge set. Pumping oilcan. Small hammer.

Consumables – in addition to those needed for maintenance you will need 5 litres Multigrade engine oil. Oil filter. Penetrating oil. Distilled water. Antifreeze.

1. Engine oil and filter change (more recent Minis or any given light usage only need have their engine oil/filter changed at six monthly, 6,000 mile intervals). 2. Fan belt tension. 3. Handbrake lever/brake pedal travel check and adjustment.

In addition to the jobs listed above, you need to carry out all of the checks listed under weekly maintenance i.e.., 1. Engine coolant. 2. Brake/clutch fluid. 3. Tyre condition and inflation. 4. Lights, electrics and washer bottle. Those who don't want to get their hands seriously dirty can have the service components carried out at their local garage and do the checks themselves – this should cost less than merely handing the car over and instructing the mechanic to 'service' the car.

If you do service the car yourself; ensure that environmentally damaging oil (and the filter) are disposed of properly. In practice, this means either keeping the oil in a large tub and – when you've filled the container – having it collected by an oil recycling company (look in your telephone directory) or – if you are on good terms with your local garage – asking them to dispose of it for you.

1. ENGINE OIL CHANGE

Unlike most cars, the Mini's engine oil is also put to use lubricating the gearbox. Oil lubricates by forming a thin layer in between two moving metal surfaces, preventing those surfaces from actually coming into contact. If oil is not present or if the oil is in poor condition,

Screen washer bottle. The more crowded engine bay of recent Minis has forced the windscreen washer bottle back into the boot.

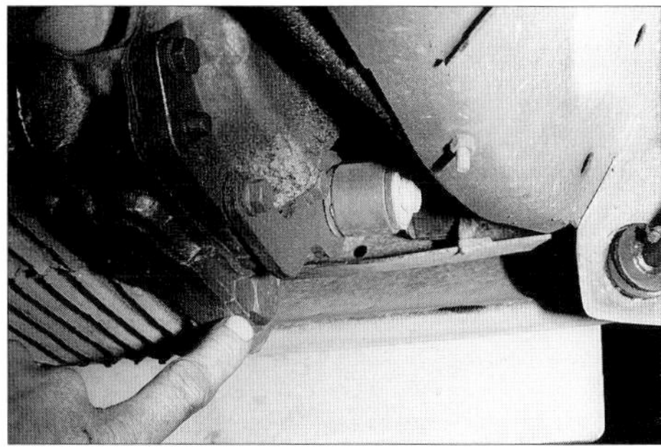

The oil sump drain plug is situated on the front off-side of the casting.

the metal surfaces will come into direct contact, and they will wear very quickly to the point at which one or both surfaces will be destroyed. Neglect the oil change and you will be rewarded with increased engine wear – in the worst case scenario, with a seized engine.

Oil also keeps the engine clean; tiny pieces of metal swarf, pieces of carbon and other potentially destructive particles within the engine are picked up by the oil which deposits them in the filter. It is essential that the oil filter is renewed at the same time as the engine oil. In addition to lubricating and cleaning the engine, the oil also plays a small but significant part in helping to keep the engine cool.

The usual recommended oil change interval is six monthly or 6,000 miles but if, like me, you tend to drive older (cherished) classic cars then by all means give the engine and gear train more frequent TLC. This is especially true of cars used mainly for short journeys.

Many people like to warm the engine through before draining away the engine oil and, indeed, this is the method prescribed by writers who have possibly never drained engine oil in their lives; the principle being that warming the oil lessens its viscosity – thickness – so that it flows more completely out of the engine and, perhaps more convincingly, that the thinned oil is better at flushing swarf down to the sump. I prefer to drain the oil after the car has been standing idle overnight – which leaves plenty of time for the oil to drain down into the sump. Whichever you choose is a matter of personal preference – I choose not to risk getting scalding old engine oil on my hands!

I clean out the sump by waiting for all the old oil to drain, then pouring a pint or two of new (cheap) engine oil into the filler and letting this, too, drain. This flushes the last of the old oil from the sump and, when you subsequently come to dip the engine, there should be clean oil on the dipstick.

To make a receptacle for the old engine oil, cut one side out of an old plastic 5 litre oil container. Place this underneath the sump drain plug, unscrew the plug and allow the oil to drain. To speed the flow of oil, remove the oil filler cap.

Because old engine oil can cause skin problems, it is as well to wear disposable plastic gloves during this part of the operation. Leave the oil to drain for at least ten or preferably fifteen minutes, so that as much as possible is drained.

While the oil is draining, attend to the filter. The filters of early cars are replaceable elements contained in a steel housing; later cars have a self-contained renewable canister which is potentially less messy to deal with! In both

Engine oil container. Cut a side out of an empty plastic 5 litre oil container and you have something ideal for draining old sump oil into. Dispose of this properly – your local garage will probably accept it for re-cycling.

To get at the ignition or oil filter, it is simplest to remove the grille – there are three self tappers per side and four across the top – unless your car is blessed with spotlights, that is.

The oil is wont to surge as it starts draining, so position the receptacle carefully.

If you cannot get the filter to turn (right) , beg the use of a strap wrench.

cases, the filter is situated on the front side of the engine but – this being the Mini – access is not terribly good.

ELEMENT FILTERS. Place a receptacle under the filter to catch the oil. Unscrew the central bolt and carefully lower the filter housing, then pour the oil away. Pull the central bolt out from the housing, noting the positions of the pressure plate, spring and washers. Wash out the housing using neat petrol or paraffin (if you use paraffin, be sure to clean all traces of it out of the housing before re-fitting it to the car).

The filter element should come in a small kit which also contains a new sealing ring and washer. Taking care not to damage the groove, prise the old sealing ring from the filter mounting on the engine, and carefully work the new ring into place. Reassemble the bolt, spring, pressure plate and washers, place the new filter in the housing, smear a little oil around the casing lip and bolt it back onto the engine. If the seal does not appear to be seating correctly, try turning the casing slightly.

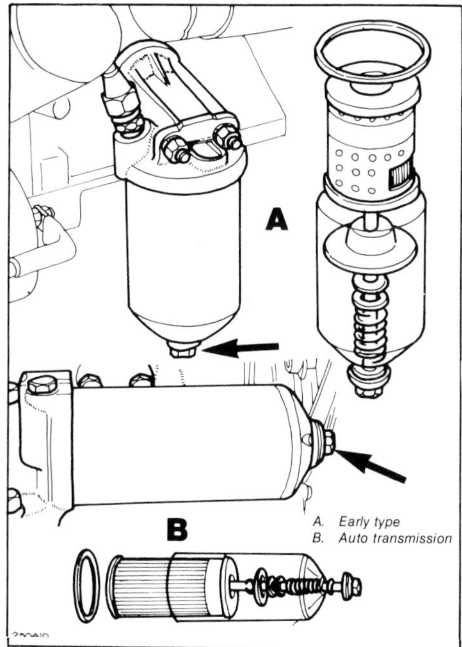

Canister oil filters. Always renew the seals along with the filter. Cartridge filters are much less messy to deal with than element filters.

CANISTER FILTER. Simply unscrew this and drain out the oil. If it proves reluctant to turn, you'll need to borrow a strap wrench – and you will find it easier to get at the filter if you unbolt the grille first. Before fitting the replacement filter, wipe a little clean engine oil onto the seal. Some people fill the canister with oil before fitting this, but the procedure recommended below renders this unnecessary.

BOTH. Before re-filling the engine with oil, I like to pour a pint or two of cheap motor oil into the engine, and allow this too to drain. As this oil drains, it starts off black and, as the last few drops drain out, it should be running clear. In effect, this is washing the tired old (often blackened) oil out of the sump for a more thorough job.

The engine oil capacity is 8.5 pints (4.83 litres). You can meter the oil out using a container of known size if preferred, or simply fill until the mark on the dipstick shows the correct level in the sump. The following advice is optional but highly recommended.

The battery *must* be in good condition (see chapter four). Remove the sparking plugs. Pull the high tension lead from the coil turret. Spin the engine on the starter motor for two bursts of ten seconds or so; this gets oil pressure up and distributes the new oil around the engine before you subject the big end bearings to the pounding they get when the engine fires up. Replace the sparking plugs and HT lead. Leave the engine for a few minutes while the bulk of the oil drains back down into the sump, then re-check the engine oil level – it will be down a little, because oil will have been pumped into the filter body – top it up if necessary.

2. FAN BELT TENSION

From 1990, all Minis have been fitted with electric engine cooling fans, though the generator drive belt is still universally referred to as the 'fan' belt. The fan belt drives not only the engine cooling fan on pre-1990 Minis but also the water pump and generator – if it becomes too slack then engine overheating will be the immediate result, followed before too long by a drained battery. Check the condition of the belt, and replace it if wear or damage is apparent. To remove the old belt, slacken the generator bracket nut and the two mounting nuts, push the generator back towards the engine – and the now-slack belt can be removed and replaced.

Check the tension of the belt by applying firm thumb pressure half-way along the longest run – between the generator and crank pulley – if the belt deflects by more than ½ in. – re-tension it by slackening off the fixings, using a large screwdriver or tyre lever to apply pressure whilst the fixings are re-tightened. Don't overdo the tensioning of the belt, incidentally, because this would place too great a strain on the generator bearings.

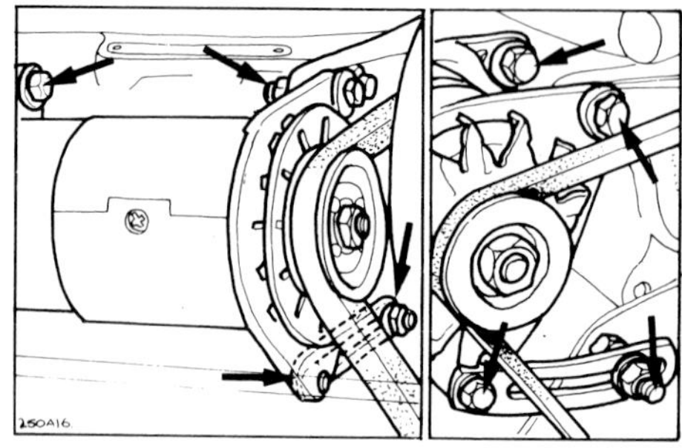

Poor battery charging from a dynamo or alternator can be due to nothing more than a slack fan belt. To adjust the tension, slacken the nuts, lever the generator and re-tighten the nuts. Don't over-do it – you'll place too much strain on the generator bearings (see text).

The alternator bolts.

3. Brake Check and Adjustment

On each of the rear brake backplates there is a ¼ in. square-drive adjuster (and two on the front brake backplates on Minis with drums at the front). When one of these is screwed in (clockwise), it forces a cone in between the brake shoes, so pushing them nearer to the drum. This has two effects – firstly, the handbrake lever does not have to rise so far until the rear wheels lock; secondly, the brake pedal travels less before operating the brakes.

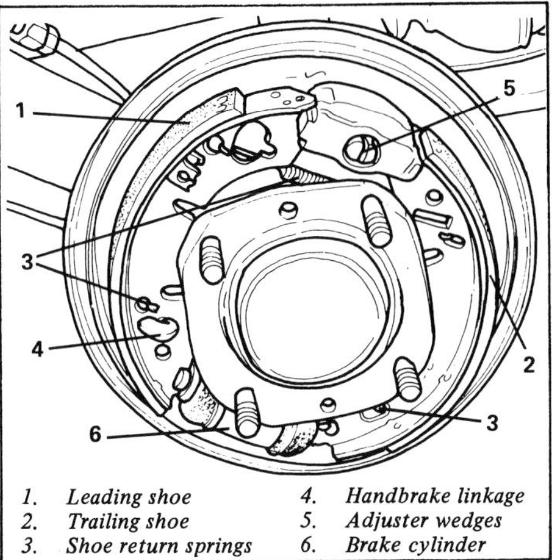

The rear brake components. Before stripping the assembly, take especial note of where the return spring ends locate.

Rear Brakes and Handbrake. Slacken the rear wheelnuts, chock the front wheels and raise the rear of the car. Remove the roadwheels. The adjuster can be seen at the top of each backplate; turn this clockwise using the proper tool until resistance is felt. Press the brake pedal to centre the shoes and re-check. The drum should turn with no drag – if there is drag, then back off the adjuster one notch and re-check. If the adjuster is seized DON'T use undue force – leave its thread soaking in penetrating oil and try later. If an adjuster proves hopelessly seized, you have to strip the brake, remove the backplate and use heat to free the adjuster (see your workshop manual) or replace the backplate complete. This is a lot of bother, so always end the adjustment by applying oil to the exposed adjuster thread.

If the handbrake lever travel is still excessive, take up the slack by turning the adjuster situated on the cable end at the base of the handbrake lever.

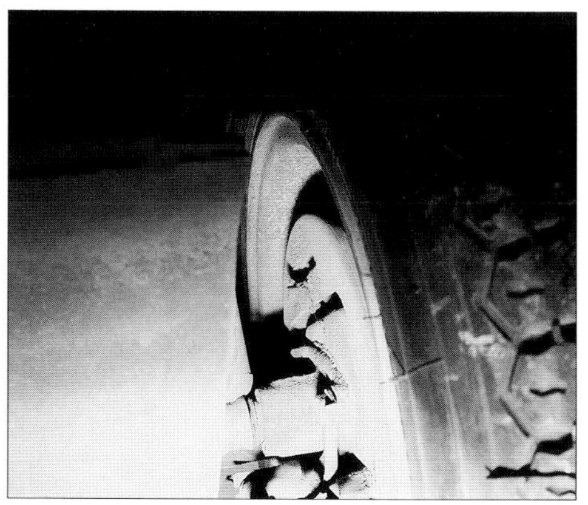

The brake adjuster is neither easy to photograph nor adjust, but it's worth moving this periodically even if the brakes don't need taking up – prevents it seizing.

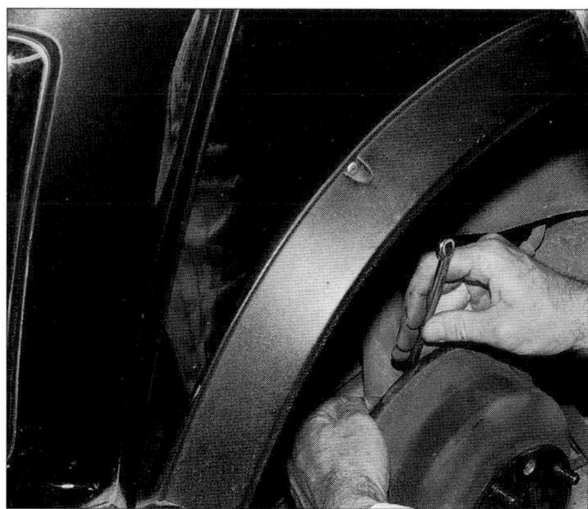

Obtain a proper brake adjuster – spanners tend to damage the square drive.

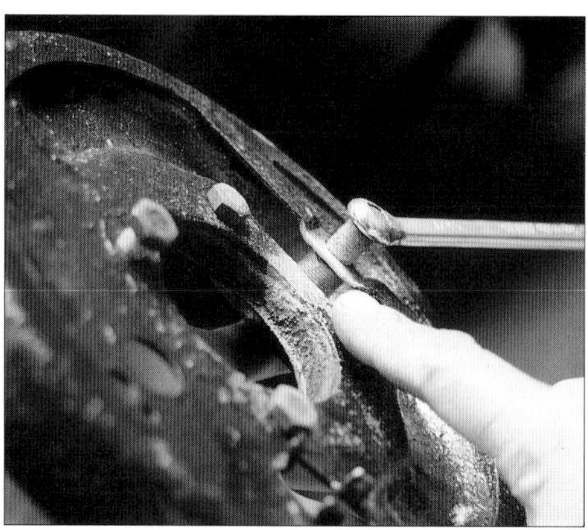

The brake back-plate is off my MG Midget, but it's essentially the same as that on a Mini. If you cannot budge the adjuster in situ, having tried soaking the thread in penetrating oil and resisted the temptation to use maximum violence, take the backplate off and use heat rather than force to free it. When it will turn a little, use lubricant and turn it forwards and back until the full range of movement is restored. I use Aluminium Anti-seize for brake adjusters – it's brilliant.

If you are losing hydraulic fluid via a wheel cylinder, any workshop manual will describe how to strip the cylinder, hone the bore if necessary and replace the seals – but a new wheel cylinder doesn't cost a lot, so it may be worth replacing rather than reconditioning if you're not on a tight budget.

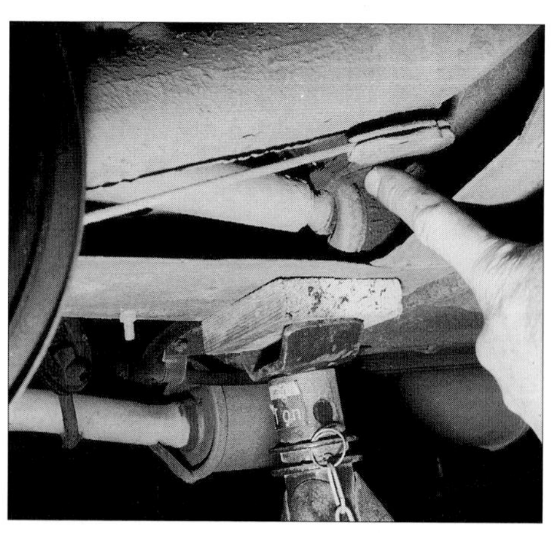

Don't forget to oil the moving quadrants.

Radius arms. It is almost traditional to discover radius arm grease nipples covered with mud, never having received any grease! Clean off the nipple, and pump in fresh grease until you see the old stuff coming out. Don't waste that old grease, smear it on the subframe – it's a great rust preventative.

If the handbrake is ineffectual or seizes on, check that the quadrants (situated on top of the radius arms) are free to turn – if not, then lubricate them.

FRONT BRAKES. No adjustment is needed for front disc brakes. Minis with drum brakes at the front have to be adjusted as already described – the only difference being that each

Front suspension arm. Another oft-neglected grease nipple. It never ceases to amaze me how even people who happily spend a fortune on Mini suspension goodies can still fail to attend to such basic maintenance jobs as giving this a few pumps with a grease gun.

shoe in the front brake assembly will have a separate adjuster.

SERVICE – 6 MONTHLY OR EVERY 6,000 MILES (WHICHEVER COMES SOONER)

Carry out all of the checks, adjustments and tasks already listed.

Some of the more complicated jobs or those which require specialised equipment may be best left to a professional. Most garages are pleased to carry out specific tasks rather than a full 'service'.

EXTRA TOOLS

In addition to the previously suggested toolkit you will require the following.

Strobe timing light.

Feeler gauges.

Torque wrench.

ENGINE AND ANCILLARIES

If the engine oil and filter were not – for whatever reason – changed during the three month/3,000 mile service then it is *essential* that they are changed as a part of this service. Cars from January 1994 have a recommended 12 month service interval, but if you own such a car and use it predominantly from short journeys (under 10 miles) I'd recommend that an oil change every six months will do no harm whatever, and possibly a lot of good! (See three month service, page 61.)

Check all of the cooling system hoses and renew any which show signs of perishing, splitting or abrasion. Check the tightness of the jubilee clips on the hoses.

IGNITION

It is often cheaper to buy a complete 'ignition service kit' from a Rover Group dealer or Mini spares specialist than it is to buy only those components which are needed for this service individually.

Check the spark plug HT lead insulation for cracks, cuts and damage. Remove the spark plugs. The condition of the spark plugs can reveal various problems with the ignition, the carburation or the engine itself. The spark plug ends should be a light fawn colour.

If the ends are badly carbonned (covered with a dry sooty layer) then the fuel/air mixture has been too rich. This could be owing to the

Remove the grille to get at the ignition components. It's usually best to remove it even for an engine oil change, and you have to do it to get at the starter solenoid.

Clean around the spark plug before removing it. A speed brace should provide ample leverage to start the spark plugs – if not, they've been over-tightened, or have been in there for too long!

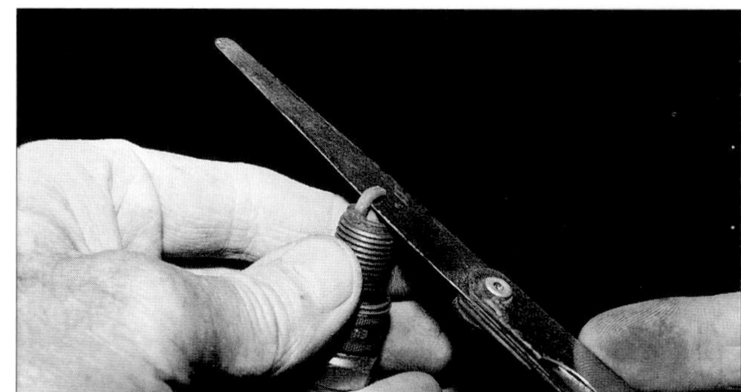

Checking the spark plug gap.

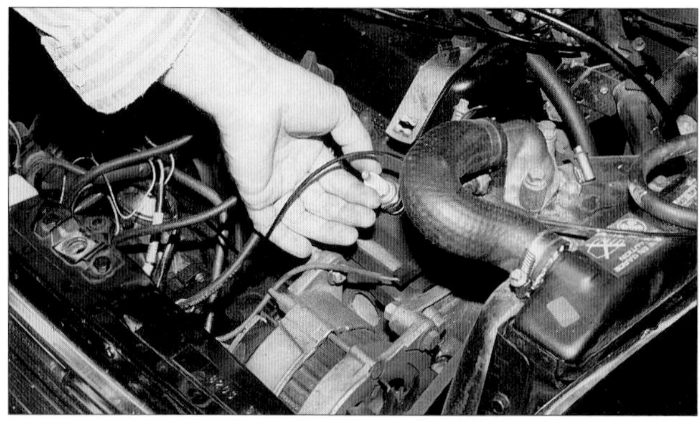

When replacing plugs, always start them by hand, so there's no risk of cross-threading them.

carburation being set badly, or to a worn jet or needle, a sticking choke cable or a clogged-up air filter. In the short term, your car will certainly have higher fuel consumption and you might experience starting problems; in the long term, the rich mixture washes oil from the cylinder bores, increasing bore and piston ring wear – the carburation needs attention. Read the rest of this chapter, chapter four and your workshop manual and, if you don't feel confident about setting the carburation or tracing the problem (if there is one!) then your local service centre will be able to help.

If the spark plugs are covered with a shiny black layer then oil is finding its way into the cylinders past the valve guide/stem or the piston rings (and burning along with the fuel/air mixture). A compression test can reveal how the oil is getting into the combustion chambers – your local service centre can test the compression for you and advise on your best course of action. Carbon or oil-covered plugs may be cleaned and re-used.

If the electrodes are burning away, if the core nose is glazed, damaged or white, then the plug is overheating for one of a number of reasons. Assuming that the correct plugs are fitted, the problem could be caused by pre-ignition, by too weak a fuel mixture or the wrong grade of fuel. Don't run the engine until you have traced and rectified the problem.

If the spark plug ends are OK, clean the electrodes thoroughly using a wire brush. Find the 0.025 in. gauge (or use two which add up to the correct thickness of twenty-five thou') and gently push it into the electrode gap. As electrodes slowly waste away, the gap will normally be slack and should be adjusted using the correct tool until the gauge can be moved within the electrode gap and only slight resistance felt. Finally, check that the screw barrel fittings on the ends of the plugs are tight. If these are loose, electrical losses can reduce the spark power, causing cold starting problems.

Remove the distributor cap by pressing onto the centre of each fixing spring and simultaneously lifting away the end. Examine the inside of the cap for cracks or black lines (carbon – which can redirect the HT energy away from the spark plug, leading to rough running and starting problems). If any cracks are found then renew the cap, because moisture in the crack from condensation will cause the HT charge to short to earth. Examine the four metal contacts for signs of damage and replace the cap if necessary. Remove the rotor arm and examine the blade for fouling. Renew the rotor arm if the blade is loose.

Examine the contact breaker points for wear and cleanliness. The contacting surfaces should not be pitted, level and clean. If a little gentle cleaning with an emery cloth will not repair the surfaces then it is safest to replace the points. Lubricate the advance/retard mechanism, the cam and the contact breaker pivot.

Points gap

Select fourth gear, disengage the handbrake and ensure that the ignition switch is 'off': push the car slowly backwards and forwards until the contact breaker arm heel is positioned on one of the cam lobes so that the points are fully open. Check the points gap using a feeler

The contact breaker points and adjustments for the 25D4, 45D4 and Ducellier distributors.

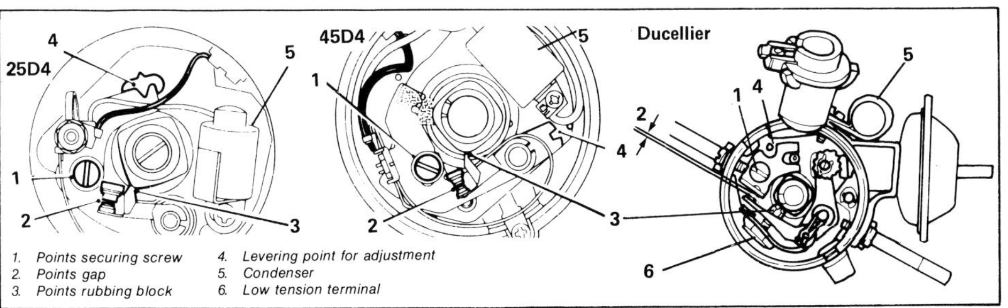

gauge, and if the gap is too large or too small then slacken the screw which holds the plate and adjust the gap by levering the plate with a small screwdriver inserted into the notch adjacent to it. If the points gap is altered then the ignition timing must be re-set. This may be carried out either with the engine running – 'dynamic' timing – or with the engine idle – static timing.

Static timing

Remove the distributor cap. The number one cylinder (nearest the radiator) should be on its compression stroke. This may be checked by removing the spark plug and turning the engine over by hand until the cylinder shows compression, or by removing the rocker box cover and turning the engine over until number one cylinder's valves are closed (rocker in uppermost part of travel) – the rotor arm will then be pointing towards number one cylinder HT lead terminal. Slacken the distributor clamp pinch bolt.

The points at this stage should be starting to open. This can be checked by switching on the ignition (do not leave the ignition turned on for too long, because you can eventually burn the coil out) and by fitting a 12V test bulb across the low tension lead and earth (the bulb will light as the points separate) or by turning on the radio and tuning it just off-station – a crack will be heard from the speaker as the points separate.

Ensure that the timing marks are correctly aligned. The timing marks vary according to the year and model. On later models they are on the timing cover next to the crankshaft pulley, on early models they are under the inspection cover plate in the clutch housing – and you ideally need a mirror to see them. Rotate the distributor until the bulb lights and fix in that position by tightening the clamp bolt.

Turn the crankshaft through a complete revolution and check that the bulb lights at the correct moment indicated by the timing marks.

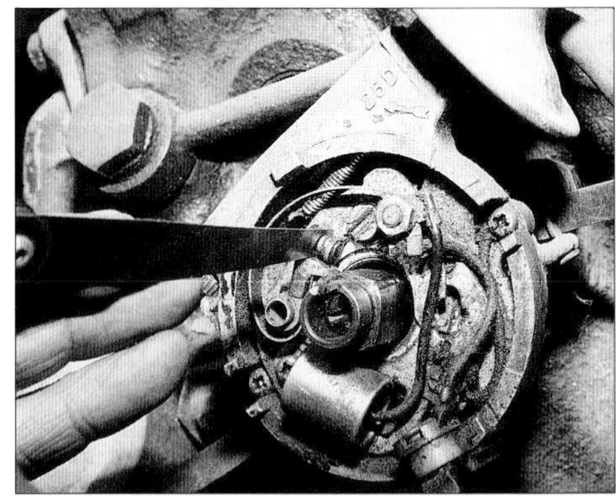

Checking the contact breaker points gap.

Slacken this set screw to adjust the gap.

Use a screwdriver to adjust the gap.

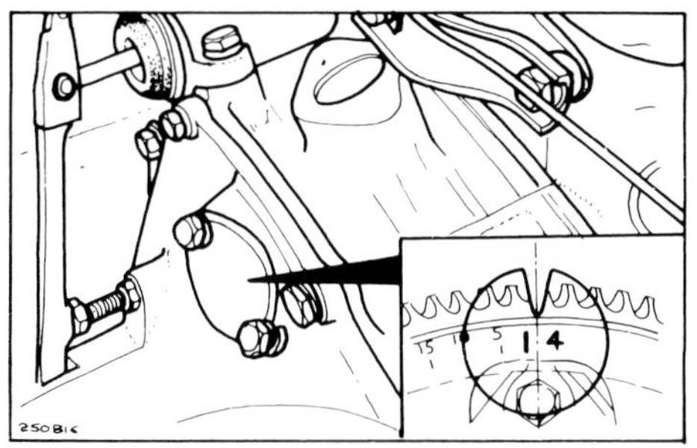

Another of those jobs which is more awkward on a Mini than most cars is dynamic timing early cars with flywheel timing marks. After removing the cover, you'll probably have to use a mirror to see the marks.

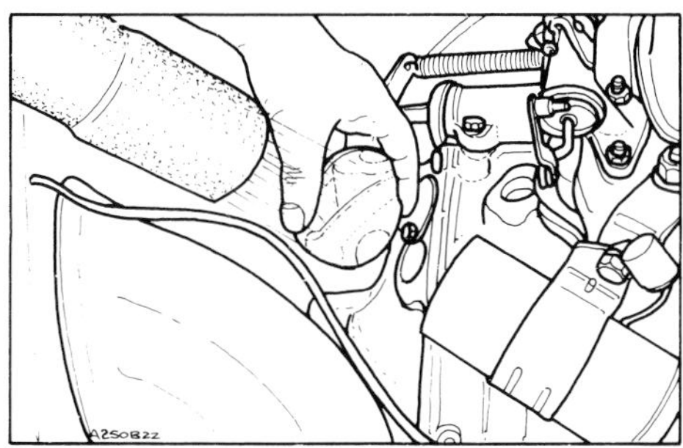

All done with mirrors. Highlight the appropriate timing marks with white paint or typist's correction fluid, or you'll stand no chance of seeing the marks.
(All diagrams courtesy Autodata)

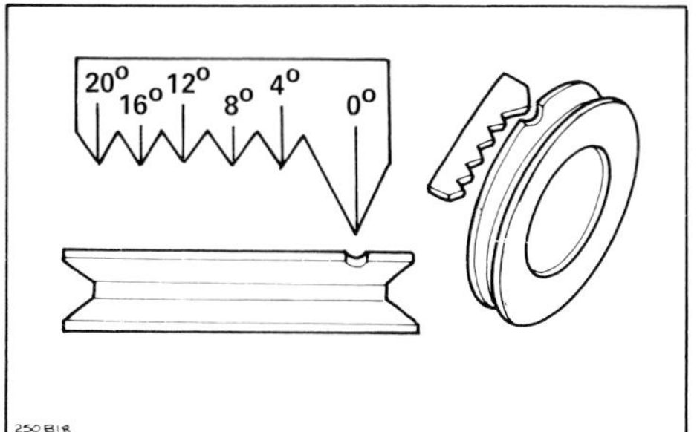

Owners of later models have an easier life, with timing marks thoughtfully placed on the crank pulley.

If it lights too early then the ignition is advanced; too late and it is retarded. Take the car for a test run and try climbing a slope on alight throttle setting or accelerating from 30 mph in fourth gear – if the engine pinks then the timing is slightly too far advanced. Small adjustments may be made using the distributor vernier adjuster (where fitted).

Dynamic timing

This requires a stroboscopic timing light, which won't cost a lot, and a bottle of typist's correction fluid is also very useful for highlighting the crankshaft pulley notch and relevant timing mark to aid visibility. Connect the stroboscopic timing light to the number one spark plug and its lead and disconnect the vacuum advance pipe, and ensure that the leads cannot become entangled in moving parts.

Start the engine and shine the flashing timing light onto the rotating crankshaft pulley using a mirror. The flashing of the light will apparently arrest the motion of the pulley, and the two marks should appear static. If the marks are out of alignment, turn the ignition off and adjust the distributor as in static timing to advance or retard the ignition timing. Re-test and readjust until they align. Use the vernier adjuster for fine adjustments.

A good multi-meter will allow you to check dwell angle. A fluctuating dwell angle is due to a worn distributor.

If the engine speed is increased, the timing mark should appear to move because of the mechanical (centrifugal) timing advance gear. Reconnect the vacuum advance pipe, again increase engine revs. There should be a further advance.

A road test can be a useful final check on timing. Warm the engine, and accelerate from around 30mph in top gear. If the engine pinks then retard the ignition slightly using the vernier adjuster.

Valve Clearances

Remove the rocker box cover. The engine has to be turned over by hand; the car may be left in gear and 'rocked' backwards and forwards, or the sparking plugs may be removed, the car taken out of gear and the engine turned over by hand using the fan belt. Alternatively, raise one of the front wheels from the ground, select first gear, remove the sparking plugs and turn the engine by turning the lifted wheel.

Turn the engine until valve number 8 (farthest from the radiator) is fully open; that is, the stem has been depressed to its maximum by its rocker. When valve 8 is fully open then the gap at valve 1 (nearest the radiator) should be set. Note that the sum of the valve numbers is 8+1 (9). The sum of the valve to be checked and that which is fully open always equals nine with the four cylinder engine. Turn the engine until valve 6 is open, and check valve 3. The remaining sequence is (first number signifies open valve, second number is valve to be adjusted) 4+5, 7+2, 1+8, 3+6, 5+4, 2+7. If the gap is correct, the 0.012 in. (twelve thou') feeler gauge will enter and move but offering a little drag.

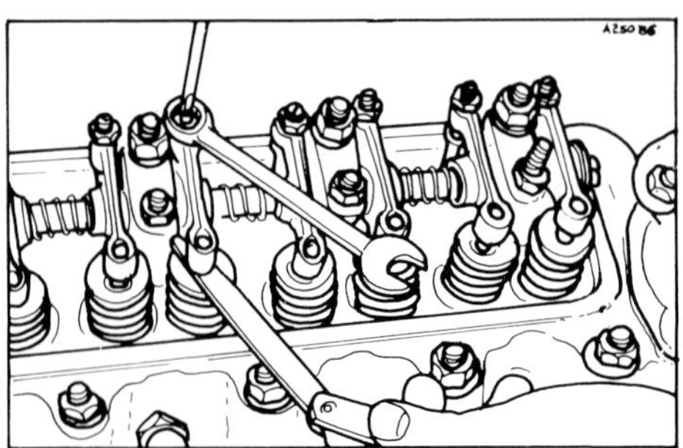

Valve gap adjustment. After slackening the nut, turn the adjuster until the feeler gauge is lightly gripped, hold the adjuster in this position with the screwdriver and pinch up the nut.

To adjust a valve if the clearance is not correct, lock the ball end screw using a screwdriver and loosen the locknut with a ring spanner. With the feeler gauge in position, gently tighten the screw until the gauge can just be moved and offers just a little resistance, and then tighten the locknut (keeping the ball end screw stationary) and recheck the gap.

Front Wheel Alignment

Because the Mini's front wheels not only steer the car but also drive it, tyre wear can be very high if the alignment of the wheels is not correct. If the front wheels are out of alignment they will be said to 'toe' in or out, meaning they will point either too far inwards or outwards, giving exceptionally high tyre wear on the outside or the inside of the tread respectively and – equally importantly, compromising roadholding. Special DIY kits are available for this, although because this is only an occasional task and a fifteen minute job for a garage or tyre fitting business, the costs of having it done professionally are low.

Do not attempt to realign the front wheels 'by eye' because this is always a mistake. If wear is apparent on one rim of the tyres do not be tempted to over-adjust the alignment to correct this, but rotate the tyres provided, of course, that the front ones are still legal.

Brakes (Drum)

With the rear of the car jacked up, clean and lubricate the handbrake cables, quadrants and compensating lever. Remove the rear wheels. Slacken off the handbrake adjuster and remove

To remove the brake drum, back off the adjuster, then remove this screw. If it is reluctant to turn, place the screwdriver in the screw head and give the screwdriver handle a sharp tap with a mallet – this usually frees it.

I prefer to clean away brake dust using a vacuum cleaner – don't breathe it in.

You have an opportunity to scribe an identification mark onto the steel part of the brake shoe. If you were to be charged for new shoes during a service, but the 'new' shoes seemed to wear after a few months' use, your mark would give you proof positive that the shoes were in fact the originals.

The wheel cylinder bleed nipple (below).

the brake drums. Check the condition of the shoes (replace if worn) and the drums (clean). The fine dust which is found in the drums might be asbestos and very hazardous to health, so wear a dust mark whilst cleaning the drums – I use an old vacuum cleaner to get rid of the dust. If the shoes have been allowed to wear too far then the drums may have been scored by the rivets, in which case they too should be renewed. Reassemble the brakes and adjust as already described. Check the condition of brake pipes, and renew any which show signs of corrosion.

Re-fit the road wheels.

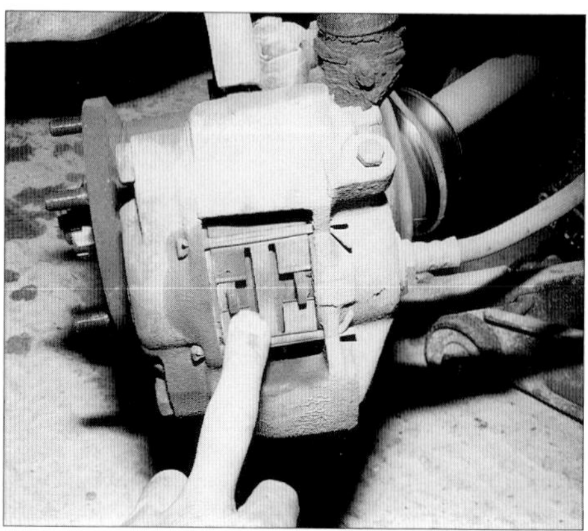

Calliper. You can check brake pad thickness visually without removing the pads. These are almost brand-new. If they are at all suspect, remove the split pins and take them out for a closer look.

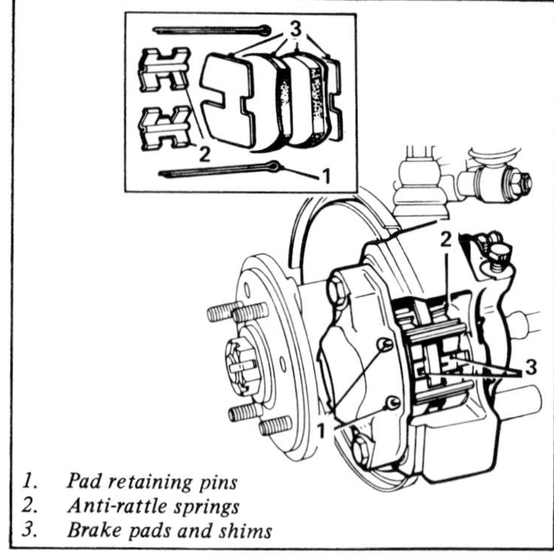

1. *Pad retaining pins*
2. *Anti-rattle springs*
3. *Brake pads and shims*

Removing the front disc pads.

Three stages in the life of a brake pad. New, well worn and 'I couldn't stop in time, Officer!'.

Front brake drums and shoes

Check that the amount of friction material on each shoe is greater than the minimum allowable 0.08 in. If not, renew the shoes. Examine the drums for pitting or scoring.

Cars fitted with disc front brakes: check the pad thickness (the minimum acceptable is 0.125 in., though I would replace them long before they wore this thin) and the disc for signs of scoring, heating or run-out (see your workshop manual). To remove the brake pads, simply remove the two split pins from the back of the calliper unit, and the two retaining springs and pads can be lifted away.

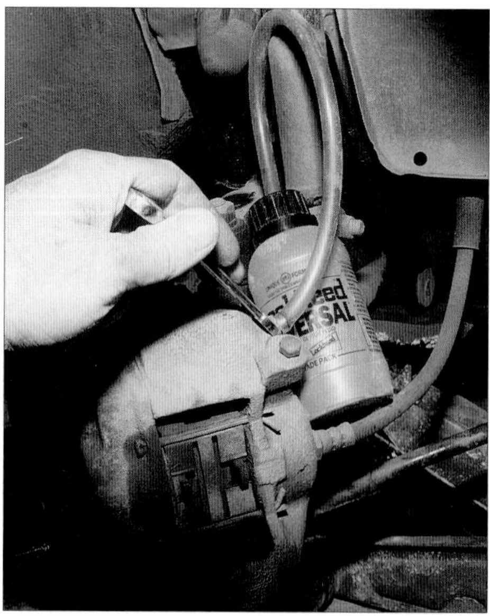

Calliper bleeding. The traditional way is with a breakable glass jar, but Clever Jim drilled a hole in the lid of an old brake fluid container, fitted the pipe snugly into this – no more spillages or smashed jars! Running the pipe uphill as I do, you don't have to worry about immersing the end of the pipe in fluid.

ANNUAL SERVICE

The annual service includes all checks and jobs listed under weekly, 3 and 6 month services.

If not previously done in an earlier service, renew the distributor cap, spark plugs and spark plug leads. I like to time the annual service so that it coincides with the MOT test.

Drain the coolant from the radiator and engine block. If the radiator does not have a drain plug then slacken the bottom hose jubilee clip. Drain the block via the drain plug (if fitted). Flush the system using a proprietary product if desired, or plain water as an alternative. Re-fill the system using the recommended quantity of new anti-freeze (not alcohol based). For temperatures down to -13 degrees Celsius use 25% anti-freeze, for temperatures down to -19 degrees Celsius use 33% and for temperatures down to -36 degrees Celsius use a 50% concentration.

Renew the fan belt and tension it so that there is a maximum deflection in the centre of the longest run of ½ in.

Check all rubber hoses in the coolant system and renew if necessary, check hoses and seals in the hydraulic brake operating system and renew if necessary. Check the crankcase breather hose for blockage and clear if necessary with a length of wire or an air compressor.

Disconnect the battery. Jack up each side of the car in turn and support with axle stands. Visually check the hydrolastic system (if fitted) for damage to pipes or displacement units; otherwise, visually check the hydraulic dampers for signs of leakage. While the car is raised, check the condition of the driveshaft gaiters and replace if they are cracked or split. This is an MOT test failure point in the UK, furthermore, the entry of dirt will cause rapid wear unless the gaiters are in good condition.

Examine the petrol tank, pump and fuel line for signs of leakage.

Check the steering and suspension for play. Check that the gaiters on the steering rack are undamaged, and replace if necessary. Check the clutch lever to stop bolt gap by removing the return spring and inserting feeler gauges into the gap.

To adjust, slacken the lock nut and screw the bolt in or out until the correct clearance is obtained, then tighten the lock nut. On early cars the clearance should be .06 in., on later cars fitted with Borg & Beck clutches .02 in., and on cars fitted with the Verto clutch .26 in.

Carburettor

Later carburettor Minis were equipped with a catalytic converter (generally abbreviated to 'cat'). This device is situated in the exhaust system, and converts certain harmful engine emissions into harmless substances. The cat will be destroyed if leaded petrol is used or if the mixture strength is too rich. For this reason, it is recommended that alterations to the carburettors of cat-equipped Minis are carried out only by professionals.

Remove the air filter. Remove the bell housing from the carburettor, carefully withdraw the piston, examine the needle for ridges, and the jet for wear (if the needle has a wear ridge or the jet is worn into an oval then they should

Happily, air filter removal is a doddle. Take care when replacing it not to disturb any of the wires or hoses/pipes which surround it.

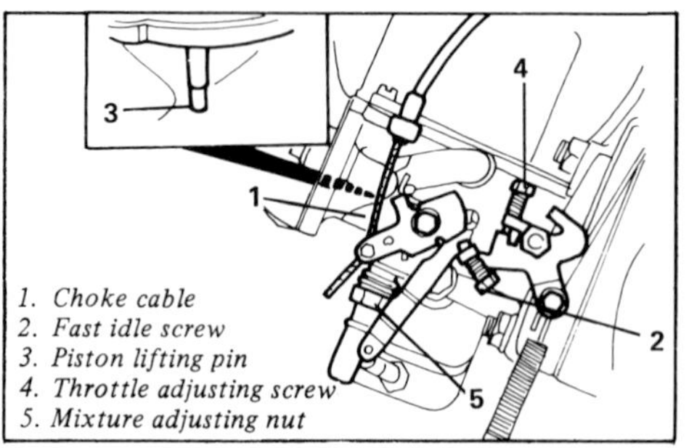

The HS2 carburettor idle adjusters. The fast idle screw (2) adjusts tickover with the choke engaged. I would advise that any alterations to the mixture adjusting nut (5) are made with the assistance of exhaust gas analysing equipment.

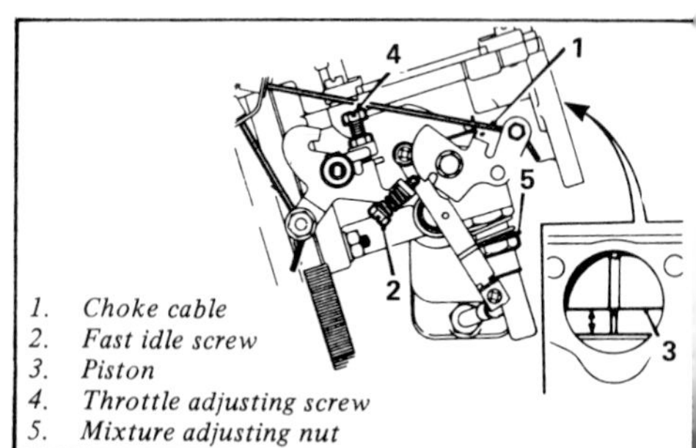

The HS4 is a larger unit. The fast idle screw (2) adjusts tickover with the choke engaged. Again, exhaust gas analysers allow accurate mixture setting.

be replaced as a set). Check that the piston is free to rise and fall (that the jet is centred and that the piston is not sticking in the bell housing). Any workshop manual will give details of how to centre the jet; if the piston is sticking in the bell housing, try cleaning both off using neat petrol and, if the problem persists, replace the two as a set. Check the mixture. You can obtain various equipment which will enable this to be carried out more accurately (exhaust gas analysers, or colour-tune spark plugs), although the following procedure can give fairly accurate settings.

Examine the exhaust tail pipe. If the inside is covered with black soot then the car is running rich, if it is a light grey then the carburation could be too lean, but could equally be OK. Check the mixture by lifting the carburettor

The Gunson's gas tester is a boon to the DIY mechanic for the task described above .

The mixture can be set spot-on with a Crypton – and this only takes a couple of minutes!

piston (using the lifting pin) while the (fully warmed) engine is at tickover. It will be necessary to remove the air filter housing to gain access for this. If the mixture is too rich then the revs will pick up when the piston is lifted, if it is too lean then the revs will immediately die away. When correctly set, the revs will pick up momentarily and settle back to the norm.

To enrich the mixture, the jet adjusting nut should be turned clockwise (looking from the top) to pull the jet downwards, and vice versa. Only turn the jet adjusting nut by a single flat at a time, and on the twin carburettor Cooper S you should begin by balancing the carbs, then adjust the mixture; work firstly on one carburettor, then the other, then the first and repeat this until the correct effect is achieved by lifting either piston. Balancing a twin carb set-up is really the province of the workshop manual, but briefly, bring the engine to normal running temperature, disconnect the linkage so that the two carbs are able to function independently, then use a length of hose to listen to the rush of air into each carburettor throat. Use the idle adjusting screws to adjust the air flow until both sound the same, and then re-clamp the linkage. You can obtain small vacuum gauges to more accurately measure the air flow.

Even the most avid DIY enthusiast would be well advised to have the twin carburettors of the Cooper S professionally jetted (tested and fitted with the most appropriate jets), balanced and set, and even those with single carburettor cars are advised to have the mixture professionally set – any MOT testing station will be able to do this.

Fuel Injection

Fuel injection systems retain a residual pressure of 25 psi or greater even after the engine has been switched off and, for reasons of safety, ON NO ACCOUNT should you tamper with the fuel injection. If you suspect any problems with the fuel injection system, check out the ignition system (the usual culprit) and, if you can find no fault with this, take the car along to a Rover dealer or a fuel injection specialist.

EVERY TWO YEARS

Renew the brake/clutch fluid, unless you have previously filled the systems with silicon fluid – if not, consider doing so now!

The clutch bleed nipple is that black smudge in the middle of the picture. (Sorry, but it's just not a very photogenic subject.) Bleeding the clutch is carried out in exactly the same manner that the brakes are bled.

BODYWORK

Most elderly Minis either have some degree of bodyrot or have had bodyrot which has been made good by the use of repair or replacement panels or – unfortunately and not uncommonly – which has been covered with a welded-on steel plate or camouflaged with body filler. There is no need for a car body to deteriorate in this manner if it is properly looked after.

General bodywork maintenance comprises regularly washing the car and waxing the paintwork so that it repels water – modern car shampoos both wash and wax at the same time and are recommended. Before washing the paintwork, however, clean mud from within the wheelarches and from the sills using a garden hose and preferably a stiff broom head. Wash as best you can the mud from the rear subframe, and ensure that the sill drain holes are not blocked. If the paintwork is dull, it can usually be lightly cut back (T-Cut or similar) and polished to a shine. Modern colour-enriched polishes in the experience of the author appear to work well, disguising small scratches, as well as scroll marks made during paint preparation.

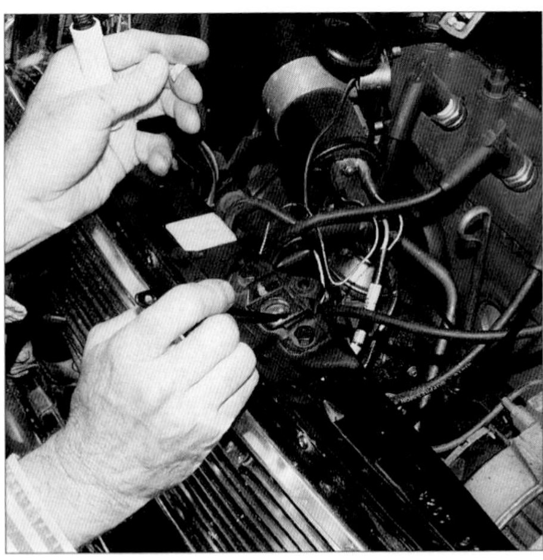

These little combined paint containers/brushes are great for dealing with minor paint blemishes, less likely to get knocked over than a paint tin.

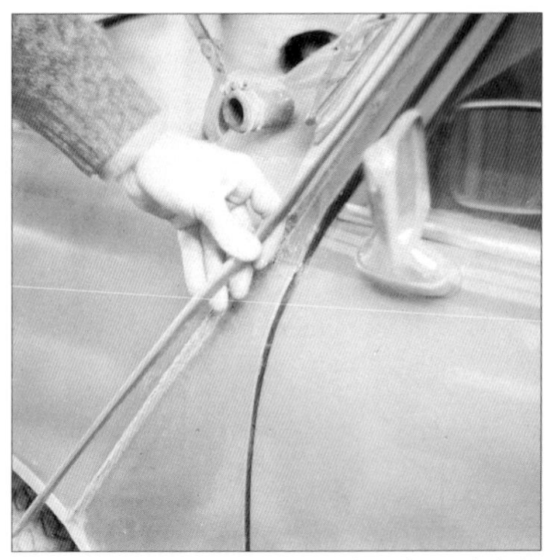

The Mini's external seams rust quietly underneath their covers on older cars. No bad thing to remove the cover, clean and paint the seam, then apply wax to the inside of the cover before gently re-fitting it.

The Mini bodyshell is manufactured from steel which, if it is allowed to come into contact with moist air, will quickly rust – that is, the surface will oxidise. In order to prevent this, car manufacturers place various coatings on car bodyshells; some are galvanised (given a coating of zinc which is very tough and which bonds to the steel), but most make do with paint. If bright steel is painted then it should not rust, but when the paintwork is breached, watch out!

Any small scratches which go right through to bright steel should be treated at the earliest opportunity – even painting on a touch of primer using a small artist's brush will afford some protection until the repair can be attended to properly. Very shallow scratches can sometimes be topcoated in the same way – brush on three or four coats (cellulose – a couple of coats will do with synthetic paint) of topcoat, allow this to harden – preferably for six weeks – then use one of the proprietary cutting

Pumping a wax (Dinitrol) behind the rear subframe, onto the heelboard end. Note the container to catch surplus wax which drips off.

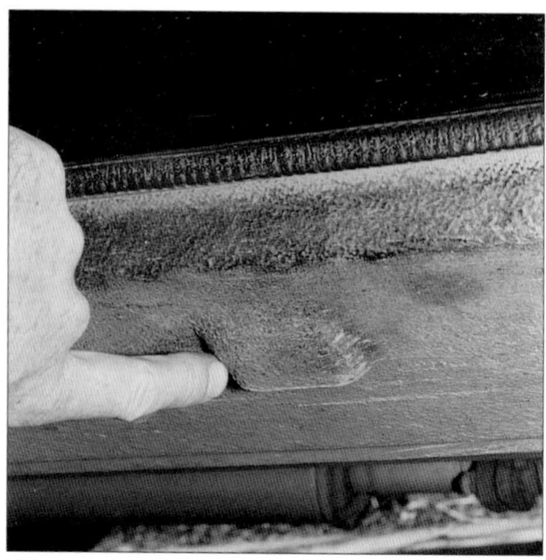

When you've injected the sills with wax, make certain that the drain holes aren't blocked up.

Wheelarch spats look smart, but rust can form underneath them, unseen. I've worked the wax injecting tube under the spat. In time, I'll get around to drilling out the spat fixing pop rivets, and inject the topside as well.

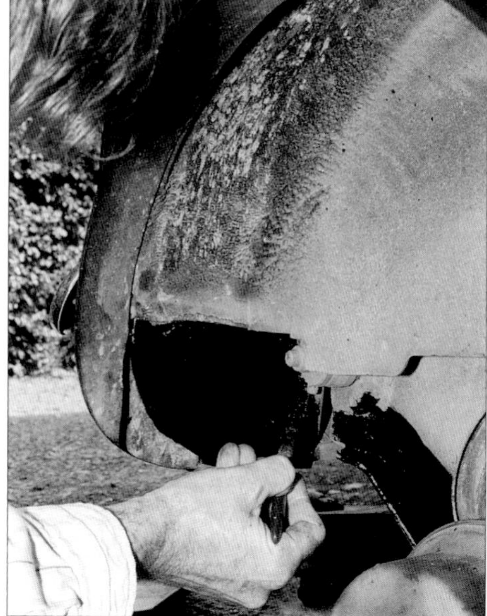

I had some old wax which had congealed; rather than throw this away, I brush painted it onto the valance closing panels.

Ideally, you'd drill a ⅜ in. hole in the valance end closing panel (being replaced here) and inject some wax. If you do drill holes for this purpose, fit a rubber bung afterwards, to keep water out.

compounds on repair and surrounding area.

Larger scratches should have their edges 'feathered'; that is, the hard shoulder should be gently sanded out. Then primer can be applied by brush or spray, followed by topcoats.

PREVENTION – BETTER THAN CURE

If your Mini is fairly recent or (perhaps following a restoration) has excellent bodywork, you can preserve the bodyshell by the application of various water repellents. Most people use proprietary wax-based products for this. These can be brushed onto many surfaces, and applied inside box sections such as the A and B posts and sills using various pumping or spraying devices. Waxes like these are messy, but nothing in comparison with some of the 'home-brewed' alternatives, which include old sump oil mixed with creosote, and oil mixed in with waxes. In truth, anything which clings to a surface and repels water will do the job.

The most important areas for treatment are enclosed box sections. As the temperature of the air within box sections warms more quickly than some parts of the steel which encloses it, moisture condenses out of 'thin air' onto the surface of the colder steel. This explains why the sills and the bases of the A and B posts are so prone to rot from the inside out. In fact, condensation can affect all steel components of the car in the same way when the air is moist and its temperature rises.

Most box sections have some form of hole through which a pipe connected to a pumping device can be inserted for the injection of rust preventatives. This might be a drain hole (which, incidentally, must NEVER be allowed to become blocked) or a hole fitted with a bung of some sort. If you can find no suitable hole, try to drill one in an area which is out of sight, and after squirting in the wax, plug it with a rubber bung.

SURVIVE THE MOD CRAVING

Before carrying out any modification to your Mini, reflect that the standard Mini usually sells more readily and realises a higher value than modified – especially DIY modified – cars. Some modifications are reversible; that is, it is an easy matter to return the car to standard specifications afterwards, and these have obvious attractions in comparison with irreversible mods, some of the more radical of which can make the car almost unsellable.

The Mini has never by contemporary standards offered much in the way of luxury for its occupants – early cars were positively Spartan inside, and it is only on relatively recent or upmarket variants that the interior becomes really welcoming. There is much that can be done to improve matters, but be warned that there is a fair quantity of junk on the market which is best avoided. In terms of the availability of bolt-on 'goodies' the Mini comes second only to the VW Beetle – in both cases, much of the paraphernalia on offer at your local motor factors is at best of questionable worth, and some of it is so dubious that it could be described as "a searing indictment of the capitalist free market economy. (Friedrich Engels, 1820-95).

Early cars are especially basic in terms of creature comforts but, before ripping out that austere trim and chucking in something more sumptuous, do stop to consider that a major part of the charm of the early Mini *is* its primitive interior. If what you want is comfort, why not sell the car to someone who will appreciate it for what it is – and buy a more recent model which gives you the cosseting you crave?

On the other hand, almost from the off, and certainly by the time the Mini began to carve a niche for itself in the rally world, boy racers with 850 Minis were busy bolting all manner of goodies into their pride and joy, and so seen in this light the quite heavily customised early Mini can be seen as an historically 'correct' car. If you want to turn your 1960s Mini 850 into a re-creation of a 60s replica Cooper, no-one has any 'purist' right to criticise your efforts.

POWER MAD

Some want show, others crave 'go', and the market offers many thousands of bolt-on performance extras for the Mini, ranging from straight-cut gear clusters (with a useful extra ratio for more relaxed motorway cruising), cross-flow eight port cylinder heads and blown engines down to go-faster stripes, or humble wheel spacers and fairly tacky plastic spats to tempt you.

In theory, any modification which alters the engine power or the handling/roadholding and hence the potential speed of a car, should be reported to the car's insurer – and the premium usually rises as a result, which temps some to fail to disclose said modifications. *Big* mistake! If the car is involved in an accident, an insurance assessor will examine it, and these chaps are unbelievably good at sniffing out *any* undisclosed modification which might invalidate the policy and hence relieve the insurer of any obligation to shell out. The result could cost you not only your car but also whatever compensatory sum a judge decided the other party deserved, and the sky is the limit!

Many of the cars on our roads would show a modest performance increase merely from being correctly set up; having the ignition timing and mixture checked on a Crypton or similar could make quite a marked difference to a sluggish Mini. A Crypton can also highlight faults with the distributor, other ignition faults which degrade the spark as well as, of course, giving an experienced operator all the clues needed to track down carburation faults such as air induction, worn needle and jet or a sticking carb piston. So, if you don't think your Mini is as fast or the engine as responsive as it should be, start with a Crypton tune.

The very first step in uprating an engine is to allow it to breathe more freely by fitting free-flow air filter(s) and a larger bore exhaust. The gain might be in the order of just 3 or 4 bhp but – if your Mini is an 850 or 1000 – this can be significant.

Serious performance modification is outside the scope of this book, but what I will say is that the average owner of a strictly road-going Mini who wants to give the car a bit more DIY 'go' is advised to give serious consideration to a simple engine transplant from 850 to 1000, from 1000 to 1100, 1275 or even 1340, rather than get too involved in fitting high-lift cams, gas-flowed heads, cross-flow heads, electronic fuel injection and the like.

Swapping the engine for a standard larger unit gives a small but significant power increase which manifests itself not so much in searing acceleration as in mid-range 'grunt' which makes overtaking manoeuvres safer. Equally importantly, it achieves that small power increase without changing the character of the car in the least, which is more than can be said

If the usual modifications are a shade too conservative for your tastes, why not consider a Mini-based kit car? Rather than chop and de-seam their old Minis, some folk opt to build themselves a Minus kit car. Members of Worcester Mini Owners' Club debate how best to plumb in an inlet manifold heater.

Perhaps inspired by the Moke, there have been a number of Mini-based kit cars which at least look as though they are intended for off-road use. This is my favourite – the Nomad – which can be assembled as a van, cab pickup, estate or open car, and which is constructed with aluminium body panels on a galvanised chassis. Best of all, the Nomad looks good with the hood up – something which cannot be said of many kit cars.

for heavily modified power units. While on the subject of swaps, a small power increase can be achieved by swapping the cylinder head – one from the 1100/1300 range in place of the standard 1,000 cc head – or by having the standard head modified; with the chamber and ports re-profiled.

Extracting more power from an engine of a given capacity usually results in some deterioration in low-end tractability, and the most heavily (professionally) modified cars can be a real pain to drive in traffic. DIY modified cars are likely to prove much less well-behaved in public so, if you want to be the fastest kid on the block then seek professional help; leave the fancy stuff to the people who know what they're doing.

A company which specialises in modifications specifically for the Mini such as the Mini Spares Centre or Mini Sport (to name but two) is as good a place as any to begin a quest for more performance. These are not the only

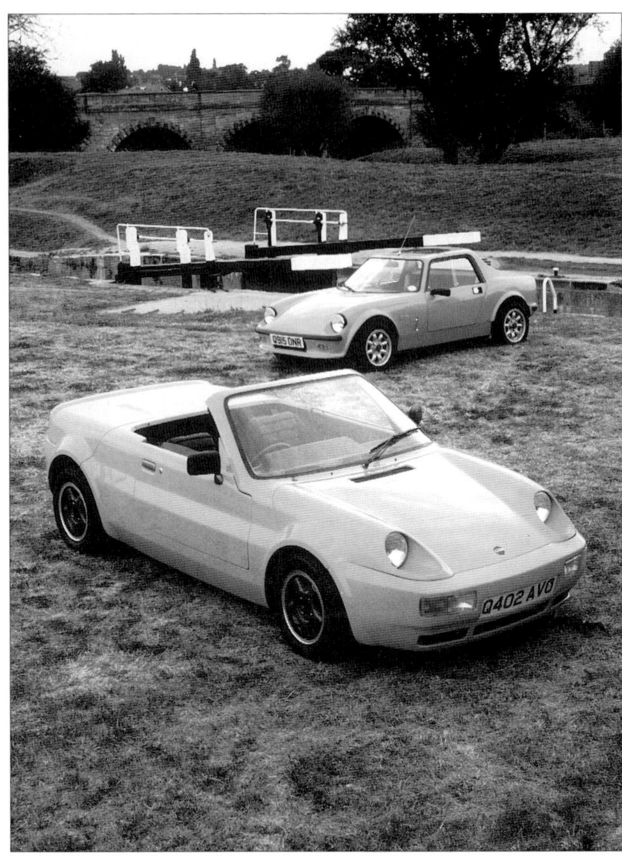

Can't afford a new MGF? Never mind, there's always the mid-engined GTM Rossa. It is nearly thirty years since the first Mini-based, mid-engined kit car (the Miura). Die-hard Mini enthusiasts might not like the idea of Minis being turned into something so obviously not a Mini, but personally, I'd rather see a Mini reborn as a kit car than go off to the crusher.

companies whose staff not only sell spares, but also race their own Minis – putting their Mini where their mouth is, so to speak – but they also produce some excellent literature on the subject of making the Mini go faster. Mini Spares Centres *Mini Tech News* is a periodical where new product promotions take second place to some very informed yet down to earth editorial features.

Novices may initially struggle with some technical and other jargon (most of which is unavoidable, a little of which is gratuitous and some merely hip), but reading publications like this (Mini Sport have also launched one and, of course, *Mini World* is a good source of up-to-date info) will give you a grounding so that when you come to consult a specialist you'll both be speaking the same language(!) and you will have a clearer understanding of what you require and how to achieve it.

On the subject of jargon, never be beguiled by anyone simply because they display an easy fluency in jargonese. Lots of people know all the theory and have developed a vocabulary which includes every technical term known to technophile man – yet absolutely no practical experience to back it up. I have known people who could hold a conversation on almost any technical aspect of car performance conversions, but who have to take their own car to a professional mechanic for any job more complicated than pumping up the tyres. They are called 'anoraks'. Their experience is nil and their advice is generally worthless.

Finally, you can bolt on hundreds, if not thousands of pounds' worth of engine go-faster goodies yet, if the fuel delivery and ignition are not spot-on, find that the car is not only less tractable than before but also slower and thirstier! Budget at the very least for a session on a Crypton or similar or, if the modifications are radical because you crave maximum BHP, on a rolling road. This won't be cheap but, if you don't have it properly set up, you might as well flush your 'go-faster goodie' money down the sump!

SUSPENSION

The standard Mini suspension – like all car suspension systems – is designed to offer a good compromise between handling, roadholding and comfort. Any alteration which improves one of these areas usually has an adverse effect on one, or both, of the others.

Before considering tweaking the suspension, stop to reflect that, in one respect, the Mini's superb roadholding could be considered its Achilles heel. Unlike its contemporaries, the Mini at its launch could be driven round corners at perhaps 99% of its potential without the driver being aware that the car was so very close to letting go of the road. Improve the suspension and you push that limit of traction further, but never lose sight of the fact that it is still there – exceed it, and you will simply have a higher speed accident.

Suspension – Wheels and Tyres

In truth, the only people who really need to upgrade the suspension of the Mini are those who wish to drive at racing speeds because, at anything other than highly illegal speeds on the public highway, the Mini will take just about anything the average driver can throw at it. The most popular – because it is easy to carry out – modification, is to fit wheel spacers. The small gain in traction on cornering which can result is to my mind offset completely by the higher stresses placed on the wheel bearings and, if you *do* fit wheel spacers, remember that the wheels and tyres must not stick out beyond the bodywork, so you'll also have to fit wheelarch spats. You can – if you wish – fit wider than standard tyres to standard rims, but again, this practice is not recommended.

Wider wheels are also a popular modification, if only because fitting them is a simple bolt-on job and because they make the Mini look a tad more aggressive. The same drawbacks as wheel spacers – the wheel bearing stresses and bodywork clearance – apply.

People who fit wider wheels and tyres usually do so in the belief that the area of contact twixt rubber and tarmac must be increased. In fact, the tyre/road contact area is governed by two factors – car weight and tyre pressure – regardless of the width of the tyres. If a car weighs 1,000 lbs (to keep to round figures) and the tyre pressure is 25 psi, then the contact area will be 1000 divided by 25, or 40 square inches – 10 square inches per tyre. The only way to increase the contact area is to increase the weight of the car (not a good idea) or to reduce the tyre pressure – a reduction to 20 psi would give a total contact area of 50 square inches – again, not a good idea. Under-inflated tyres wear very rapidly at their outer edges but – more importantly – the air pressure is in effect an air 'spring' and as such is a fully functional component of the suspension.

Unlike the suspension, however, the air spring is un-damped, and the recommended tyre pressures have been calculated to give the optimum in handling and roadholding. Trust Mister Issigonis' recommendations – he was right about everything else! Change tyre pressures and you change the handling and roadholding capabilities.

If you are determined to fit wider wheels and tyres, my advice is to consult and buy from one of the recognised Mini performance spares specialists, and to seek their advice not just on wide wheels and tyres, but on the suspension as a whole. Do bear in mind that full competition suspensions have a number of drawbacks if fitted to a road-going car.

There is another consideration to fitting wide wheels etc., which is that by making your Mini appear a street racer, you are throwing down a gauntlet to every driver of more recent faster machinery. A GTI or similar will make mincemeat of all but the most highly modified Minis, and some of the drivers of faster modern cars love rubbing what they see as lesser mortals' noses in it.

Suspension – Other Mods

As with engine modifications, if you wish to modify your Mini's suspension, my advice is to seek professional advice and use proprietary products from a Mini specialist. Even then, it is well worth having the suspension professionally checked over before using the car on the road. DIY lash-ups are at best questionable even on a car driven at normal speeds – on a car which is intended for high-speed use their adoption verges on lunacy.

If you've a deep enough pocket and wild enough ambitions, there are a lot of radical Mini suspension mods to part you from your cash. Variable ride height suspension is one of the more interesting and one which can be of real worth for road-going cars, because it allows you to lower the car for fast progress on smooth tarmac and to raise it if you wish to go off-road, or even up a bumpy rural driveway which would punish the sump of the standard Mini. The kits replace the standard aluminium cones with alternatives with variable length and which are altered by use of a spanner or key – one corner of the car at a time. Fitting the kits is definitely a job only for the more experienced DIY mechanic, though.

Ride height can also be altered by shortening or packing the suspension trumpets (cones); the ratios being 3:1 front. 5:1 rear. If you were to shorten the front cones by ⅓ in., for instance, the front of the car would be lowered by 1 in. – and vice-versa.

Negative camber – when a wheel slopes inwards at the top – improves cornering grip (though at the expense of greatly increased tyre wear) and is a favourite and proven modification for competition cars. Negative camber at the front wheels is an automatic side-effect of lowering the front end of a Mini, though negative camber suspension arms are available. Negative camber at the rear can be achieved by elongating the radius arm bracket hole (NOT recommended) or by fitting alternative brackets, either fixed (recommended) or adjustable. You can also reduce the rear wheel toe-in (reducing understeer) by shimming the bracket.

Your typical road-going Mini hardly needs negative camber, though, because only a maniac would drive fast enough (probably at illegal and dangerous speeds) on the public highway to feel any tangible benefit.

INTERIOR

Early Mini seats are not the most comfortable and can be irksome towards the end of a lengthy journey. The temptation is to rip them out and chuck in something more supportive, and there is no small choice of after-market seats and subframes (remember to buy tipping subframes) which can be shoehorned into the Mini. A lower cost alternative is the padded seat cover; these generally offer lateral support to stop you slipping from side to side on hard cornering, plus a little lumber support which those who suffer back problems will have reason to bless.

Another alternative is to acquire and fit a pair of seats from a different car altogether. The great constraint is the limited interior width of the Mini, which means that very wide seats obviously won't fit. Measure the available width in the car, then pay your local friendly car breaker a visit and sorely tempt his wrath by going through his stock of seats until you find something which both appeals and fits. You will, of course, have to manufacture your own brackets and live with the non-matching front and rear seats.

At far greater expense, look in your local business listings for upholsterers, and have your existing seats re-covered and padded to your own specifications. This is probably the best alternative for the owner of an early Mini who wants or needs extra comfort but who wishes the car to retain the right interior look. The cost of having bespoke covers made – using the existing ones as templates – should not be too much greater than that of buying a set of off-the-peg covers and having them fitted, but the results will be in a different league. If you want real class, a professional upholsterer can work in leather as easily as vinyl!

One very simple interior improvement is to fit carpets, preferably with an underlay to further reduce road noise. The brave can order carpet on the roll and, using paper templates, cut and edge stitch them (you'll need an industrial sewing machine). Most will buy their carpets ready-tailored. The rule here is that very cheap carpets don't last very long; try to find a set with a moulded-in rubber heel area for the driver's side and they'll last a little longer. Good quality carpets are far harder wearing.

Keeping Warm

For a car so well served with uprated aftermarket componentry, the Mini spares trade seem not too bothered with the comfort factor, but concentrate their efforts almost exclusively into 'show or go' mods! In the winter when the heater is most likely to be 'on', the engine will tend to run at a cooler temperature simply because the heater radiator is operating and assisting in the cooling effort, so try fitting a higher temperature thermostat – say, 82 or 88 degrees. This will help to maintain a higher coolant temperature, and make the air coming into the cab a tad warmer.

If you suspect that your heater performance is down, then the heater radiator (matrix) could be clogged up internally, and you might experience an improvement by removing the matrix and flushing it out.

Keeping Cool

The simplest ideas are often the best. If your Mini has vinyl seat covers, there is little more irritating on a long journey in hot weather than having your shirt soaked in sweat and sticking to your back. Take one bath towel and drape it down the seat back (making sure, of course, that the it complements the interior colour scheme). It's a lot cheaper than outshining the Mini Cooper with duo-tone cream and red leather.

Sunroof

Short of fitting air conditioning or chopping the roof off, the ultimate in 'keep-you-cool' accessories is the sunroof. The ultimate sunroof is the full-length folding fabric 'Webasco' type (the powered full-length sunroof of the Mini British Open Classic must surely rate as its main attraction), though many will settle instead for one of the modern translucent plastic jobs. In either case, fitting involves accurately cutting the roof (without distorting it) and the headlining, and it is usually best to buy from a company which will also fit the sunroof. The actual fitting charge will normally be the smallest part of the total price and, considering that it is a sure-fire way to get a first class job, it is a small price to pay.

If you wish to fit your own sunroof, then I suggest investing in a nibbler; these devices fit into electric drills and 'nibble' a distortion-free ⅛ in. cut which – unlike angle grinders and air hacksaws – leaves edges which aren't as sharp as razors! Do take time to firstly go over where the cutting line will run in the roof inch by inch with a magnet to check for deep holes filled with bodyfiller or bridged with GRP – just in case the car has ever been rolled.

There are companies which, in return for a substantial wad, will strengthen your Mini shell then hack the top off. You can alternatively buy the necessary parts in a kit (which *must* include weld-in strengthening panels for the sills and scuttle/A post) and do the work yourself. If you wish to go topless and nothing but a Mini will do, this is the only sensible alternative when your pocket is too shallow for the (factory) Mini Cabriolet – priced new at around £12,000 – (a lot of money for a Mini but not for this beautifully styled, solidly built and sumptuous 'instant classic' car Unlike some third-party roof-chops, the factory Cabriolet is beautifully put together and looks superb – a real head-turner).

A topless Mini might be the ultimate in cool, but the occupants won't necessarily be cool if caught up in a traditional British Bank Holiday hottest-day-of-the-year-so-let's-resurface-the-roads traffic jam with the relentless mid-day sun beating down on them. More importantly: 1. Brainless ones with sharp knives are drawn to soft-tops like bees to a honeypot: 2. Being caught in an upside-down chopped Mini can be a terminal experience – fit a roll bar. Remember that before hacking the roof off.

STAYING DRY

Leaking windscreen rubbers are the most common source of that puddle on the floor (Paddy Hopkirk's less experienced rally partners excepted) and, although fitting a replacement rubber is the proper cure, you can sometimes effect a seal by carefully lifting the lip of the rubber (use the blunt end of a teaspoon or similar) and working in screen sealant. Wipe away any excess with white spirit and a rag before it hardens on the paintwork. If the rubber becomes old and brittle, however, replacement is the only cure. Two tips to ease windscreen fitting; use Swarfega hand cleaner as a lubricant for the rubber, and use plastic-covered wire to pull the lip into position. Windscreen replacement is covered in all workshop manuals, but be warned – fun it isn't!

IN CAR ENTERTAINMENT (ICE)

In-car entertainment (ICE) equipment is a catch-all term nowadays applied to radios, cassette players, graphic equalisers and CDs.

Those with early cars might like to try and fit a basic period radio unit which is in keeping with the general character of their car. These units can be obtained from some specialists who have (showing great foresight) rescued many such radios over the years from scrapped cars, then serviced them and placed them into storage for future sale. These radios will not be cheap and you may in fact be asked to pay more than the price of a far better modern alternative. Most breakers will have a stock of period radios taken from scrapped cars, which will be cheaper. Remember that the original design didn't even allow for a radio!

An exploded view of the heater unit. You can flush the radiator without stripping the unit.

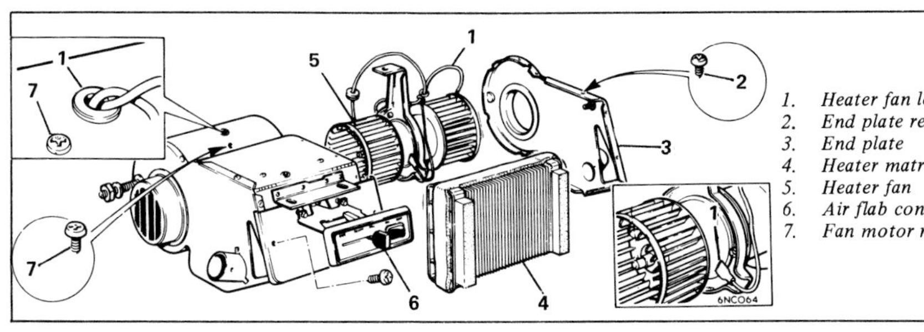

1. *Heater fan leads*
2. *End plate retaining screw*
3. *End plate*
4. *Heater matrix*
5. *Heater fan*
6. *Air flab control*
7. *Fan motor retaining screw*

Modern ICE equipment is often very different from the equivalent which might have typically been fitted to an early Mini. It is possible to hang both the central ICE unit plus a graphic equaliser underneath the parcel shelf of the car, using the standard Meccano-like strips of metal which are provided for the purpose with most of this equipment, or by fitting a centre console. The drawback is theft. Theft of modern ICE equipment from parked cars is rife. If you are in two minds whether to fit a basic unit or an expensive unit, bear in mind that thieves tend to steal only the better quality ICE equipment!

General Installation Notes

Other electrical equipment in the car can cause interference and unwanted speaker noise when the car radio is in use. In general, you should try to keep components and leads – including the aerial lead – as far away from all elements of the ignition and direction indicator circuits as possible. Check that the unit has a good earth and the correct 1 amp or 2 amp in-line fuse fitted. Also fit an in-line choke (available – as are other electrical components mentioned here – at motor factors or radio shops) in the electrical supply to the radio, preferably as close as possible to the unit.

Using carbon rather than copper cored high tension leads removes one potential source of interference and is a more elegant solution than using resistive plug caps or in-line resistors in the HT leads.

The generator and contact breaker point ignition have the potential to cause interference; fit a .1 mf capacitor between an earth and the coil positive terminal, and another in between earth and the large terminal on the generator. Electronic ignition systems have built-in suppression – don't fit a capacitor to the coil in this instance because you risk damaging the system if you do.

If, after taking the steps outlined here, interference is still a problem then there are specialist works available which may be able to help: alternatively, consult a specialist.

Lights

Spot and fog lamps can make driving your Mini safer; such units are widely available at motor factors and almost all come with fitting instructions. The important point is that any extra lamps should not draw too high a current through existing wiring, yet at the same time, it is no bad thing to wire spot and fog lamps so that they can only be switched on when the existing system is live (when the headlights are on), to prevent them inadvertently being left on to drain the battery.

The solution is to take power direct from the battery (incorporate an in-line fuse if you do this) or from a spare connector on the fuse block, but to switch this circuit on and off by means of a relay – an electrically operated switch – which draws its meagre power needs from the existing lighting circuit. Unless the lights are on, the relay won't operate and hence the extra lights cannot inadvertently be left switched on to drain the battery. Chapter four gives an introduction to auto electrics, but I recommend that extra lights are wired by an auto electrician.

Voltmeter and Ammeter

An ammeter measures all current flow to and from the battery save the 300 to 400 amp drain of the starter motor, and so it shows the state of charge or discharge. The problem with the ammeter is that very thick wiring needed to carry sometimes quite heavy currents has to be run to the meter, with all the attendant risks. A voltmeter merely shows the rate of battery charge in volts – anything less than 13 volts indicates undercharging, much more than 14, over-charging. Of the two, the voltmeter is arguably the more worthwhile.

It is, however, questionable whether the usefulness of either instrument warrants its cost – if a battery is slowly running low, you'll know because the starter motor will spin more slowly than usually; if the generator suddenly stops charging because the belt slips or breaks, the ignition light will come on.

Tachometer

It is in motorsport that the tacho comes into its own. When you need to level the revs at, say, 3000 rpm before dropping the clutch in second gear for a quick getaway for a hillclimb or sprint, you'll be needing a tacho. In normal use, a tachometer is nice to glance at occasionally, but hardly essential, and the novelty soon wears off…

BATTERY ISOLATOR

Electrical fires in old cars occur frequently enough to be a serious worry, and can reduce a car to a burnt-out shell in a matter of minutes if the fire originates close to inflammable brake/clutch fluid, petrol (the Mini's battery is in close proximity to the fuel tank!) or upholstery. I have first-hand experience of an electrical fire: it occurred behind the dashboard of my '66 MGB GT while the car was parked on my drive. It was no more than perhaps twenty or thirty seconds before the interior of the car was filled with choking fumes and, by the time luggage from the rear seat, the seat base and the battery cover had been thrown out onto the lawn so that the battery earth terminal could be disconnected, the permanently live (brown) wires concerned had burnt away the majority of their insulation.

Electrical fires start because current passes through a wire at a higher amperage (current) than the wire is able to tolerate – usually when un-insulated wire, terminals or part of an electrical component touches earth (the bodywork of the car) – without a load in the (shortened) circuit, the battery discharges at its maximum rate and the wire concerned becomes hot, then melts its insulation which eventually catches fire. Most circuits are fused – that is, they contain a special length of wire which has no insulation and which is designed to burn through safely if the current through it is higher than a pre-determined level. Not all circuits, however, contain fuses. The lighting and ignition circuits usually have none.

There is a strong case for fitting a battery isolation switch which, when operated, disconnects the earth terminal from the bodywork, so preventing current from flowing in any wires. The type of switch the Mini owner needs is that found on competition cars rather than types which fit to the battery earth post itself (the battery being situated in the boot); these can be obtained from most motor accessory shops. Again, an auto-electrician will undertake the fitting of this switch and, unless you know what you are doing, it is recommended that you take this option.

ECONOMY DRIVE

Motor manufacturers have made great progress in the fuel economy offered by their cars in recent years, yet even the 1959 Mini is still exemplary in this respect. You can, however, encourage your Mini to even greater frugality. One of the greatest aids to fuel economy is a light accelerator foot! How you drive the car has a huge bearing on miles per gallon. If you go all out for speed between the bends and brake frequently, then you can expect maximum fuel consumption.

Driving economically, however, does not necessarily mean driving slowly. It takes a great amount of energy to accelerate a car to a fixed speed, and equally as much energy to stop it from that speed! Every time you apply the brakes, you are wasting energy (in the form of burnt mixture) which would otherwise help maintain your forward momentum. So the less you can use the brakes the better (this also saves on brake wear).

Reducing use of the brakes is easier and not as dangerous as it may at first sound. The secret is to do what any good driver should and to look and think ahead at all times. Instead of braking immediately before reaching a corner, try to slowly decelerate so that the car is travelling at the correct speed when you reach it, and treat obstacles in the road, such as parked vehicles which have to be passed, in the same way. Reducing acceleration and building up speed slowly instead can also save a lot of fuel, because cars drink petrol very quickly when the throttle is fully open. In both acceleration and braking, the accent is on driving the car as smoothly and gently as possible and consistent with road safety.

On long, straight roads, you can save a lot of fuel by reducing your speed to an optimum level consistent with available travelling time and road safety. Those who have driven cars with accurate fuel flow (MGP) meters on motorways will be aware that fuel consumption per mile travelled increases alarmingly along with speed. The exact speeds at which consumption shows marked increases will vary according to the type of car, but basically, remember that sixty miles per hour is cheaper than seventy, but more expensive than fifty-five! In the case of busy 'A' roads and motorways, however, the advantages of fuel saving are outweighed by the safety factor in keeping pace with the other traffic.

Many people are taking advantage of the cost savings offered by unleaded fuel in most countries today, and although unleaded fuel should NEVER be used in the standard pre-1989 Mini it is possible to use unleaded fuel in engines fitted with modified cylinder heads. These are now widely advertised and are available as exchange items. A substantial deposit, refundable on receipt of your old engine or cylinder head, may be levied. Before swapping engines in the interests of reducing pollution, reflect that unleaded fuel allegedly gives worse emissions than leaded unless it is used in conjunction with a catalytic converter. Worse, 'cats' only operate when they have reached a high operating temperature, so that a modern cat equipped car burning unleaded fuel but used predominantly for short journeys might pump out far more dangerous pollution than a properly set-up carburettor Mini burning leaded fuel. The jury is still out on the cat.

FALSE ECONOMIES

Many gadgets claimed to reduce fuel consumption have been offered to the motorist over the years. At one time, it was possible to add up the percentage fuel savings claimed for the gadgets to over 100% so that, theoretically, if you fitted them all to your own car then it would run on fresh air!

The Trades Descriptions Act took care of some of the more ridiculous of these advertising claims in the UK, but they did not do away with the fuel-saving gadget itself. It is not possible to state with 100% certainty that none of these devices can improve your fuel economy, but readers are generally advised to spend their money on having their cars' ignition and carburation systems correctly set up and maintained rather than on fuel saving gadgetry. Even if your ignition and carburation were perfectly set up, you could waste fuel if the car's tyre pressures were too low, or worse, if the rear brakes were binding.

Driving with binding brakes is rather like constantly driving up a very steep hill, and the fuel wastage is enormous. It is easy enough to test for binding brakes. Take the car for a short run (using the brakes a little to warm them up), then jack up one corner at a time and spin the wheels by hand. Binding will be obvious. The front disc brakes (where fitted) should drag very slightly when tested in this way, but if real rolling resistance is felt then the calliper pistons are sticking and remedial action will be necessary. Drum brakes are adjustable, and slackening off the adjuster a fraction may or may not stop the binding. If not, the brake assembly will have to be stripped, freed and properly lubricated. If you have never undertaken this type of work before then either consult a good workshop manual before proceeding or have the work carried out professionally. Binding brakes can also be caused by problems with the master cylinder, or damaged brake lines – consult professionals if you have such problems.

Having too-low tyre pressures will not only increase fuel consumption, but it will also accelerate tyre wear. Do not be tempted to over-inflate the tyres to compensate, however, because this will also accelerate tyre wear and more importantly it will reduce the road-holding of the car under certain circumstances. While on the subject of tyres, the greatest cost saving you can make is not to get caught with illegal ones! In the UK, the fine *per illegal tyre* is enough to buy a complete new set of high quality tyres.

SECURITY

The modern solution to automotive theft is to fit ever-more sophisticated electronic alarm systems but, as the systems become more complex, so new means are devised by criminal types to overcome them. At the time of writing, so-called 'grabber' devices are widely available and able to decipher the electronic codes used on the most sophisticated alarm systems. To make matters worse, car alarms have such a reputation for setting themselves off (like the boy who cried wolf) that many people simply ignore the sound of a car alarm. If you wish to have an alarm in your car then the best advice is to take professional advice from your local Crime Prevention Officer and to have the device fitted by professionals.

Alternative physical anti-theft devices fare little better. Steering locks can be broken, as can many of the third-party devices which clamp on to the steering wheel, pedals, handbrake lever or a combination of these. If an accomplished and determined thief wants to steal your car badly enough, then he or she will usually succeed.

Firstly, there are security measures which you can take whenever you have to leave your car locked in your garage or parked on your driveway for any period of time – say, more than a few days. Disconnecting the battery and removing the earth strap (or even the battery) takes maybe ten minutes, removing the distributor cap and/or rotor arm takes even less time – both will stop most thieves, because few will be armed with the components which you have removed to disable the car.

So-called 'joyriders' who steal cars in order to drive them at breakneck speeds present a problem to the customised Mini owner. Although these people generally prefer the modern 'hot hatch' type of car, a nice Mini Cooper or even a Mini which looks as though it is fast will undoubtedly appeal to many. Joyriders don't steal the car for financial gain, and hence they are have no compunction in doing whatever damage proves necessary to get the engine going and the car on the move. Proprietary physical locking devices will dissuade many from attempting to take a car, but some of these devices are able to be kicked or hammered off, so choose carefully and follow the recommendation of your local Crime Prevention Officer. That's what he or she is there for.

The best way to prevent theft, in my opinion, is to dissuade the thief from stealing the car rather than trying to prevent him from doing so.

The motive for most thefts being the financial profit from the subsequent sale of the vehicle, you can dissuade the thief by marking the car's registration number onto as many components as possible. This is just a simple extension of having the registration number engraved onto the windows, but a very effective one, because at a stroke, you prevent the thief from giving the car a false set of plates and selling it, and also from breaking the car for sale as spares.

Security marking kits, containing stencils and engraving, indelible ink and other markers, are widely available and, armed with such a kit, there are few components which cannot be marked with the car's registration number.

Chapter Three

Surviving Restoration

Before starting a DIY Mini restoration project, do take time to consider whether it might be a better idea to buy an already-restored Mini instead (or even a fairly recent Mini – some of the limited edition cars from the 1980s and '90s are undeniably classics and many will be in excellent condition). Apart from any other consideration, few restored classic cars (even those restored on a DIY basis) are worth anything like as much as their combined purchase and restoration costs and, by buying a ready restored car, you will be avoiding the loss which the seller will almost certainly have to take on the deal.

Unless you already have first-hand restoration experience, it is unlikely that you really know what you are letting yourself in for when you embark on a restoration. Some people who pontificate on the subject of restoration with an authority that suggests they are the hardened veteran of a thousand restorations might not actually have any first-hand experience of restoration, their 'experience' being limited, in fact, to what they have read on the subject, or what a professional restorer has told them. Despite having their cars restored by professionals, some people claim to have done it all themselves and, having created the myth that they know what they're talking about on the subject, they have to live the lie by making things up.

If anyone tries to convince you that the Mini is anything other than hard labour to restore then treat their advice with a large pinch of salt – it is as difficult to restore as any other car in equivalent condition and the same age. Restoration is bloody hard work, and only the experienced (battle hardened?) restorer can know just how great an undertaking a complete classic car restoration is.

Most books and magazine articles on the subject deal well enough with specific skilled tasks such as welding, mechanical repair and paint spraying, but don't inform the reader that these highly skilled tasks represent a tiny fraction of the work which makes up a restoration. Most of the DIY restorer's time is spent scraping away old underseal, scraping, chiselling or otherwise cleaning away old paint, rust, grease and sundry dirt from body and components. When more skilled work comes along, the unskilled preparation usually takes many times as long as the skilled work. When you're painting a car, for instance, it takes only minutes to spray each topcoat but, in order that those few minutes' work are successful, it is necessary to spend many hours, days – sometimes weeks if you are working only evenings and week-ends – in preparation. A repair panel can be welded into position in minutes – but usually only after hours of preparation.

Don't be tempted to fool yourself that a part-restoration is any easier than a complete, stripped to a bare shell, restoration. You can start, for instance, to re-spray the engine bay sides (flitch panels) to smarten up a jaded engine bay. This firstly involves stripping out the bay and, as you remove the many and varied components you will discover that many need replacement or at the very least a thorough cleaning followed by re-painting. Many components will be damaged as you remove them – or more usually their seized fittings will shear and have to be replaced. The costs continue to mount.

As you strip paint from the panels you will usually find some areas of rot which have to be cut out and have new steel welded in. The problem then is recognising when to stop, because a newly painted engine bay makes the

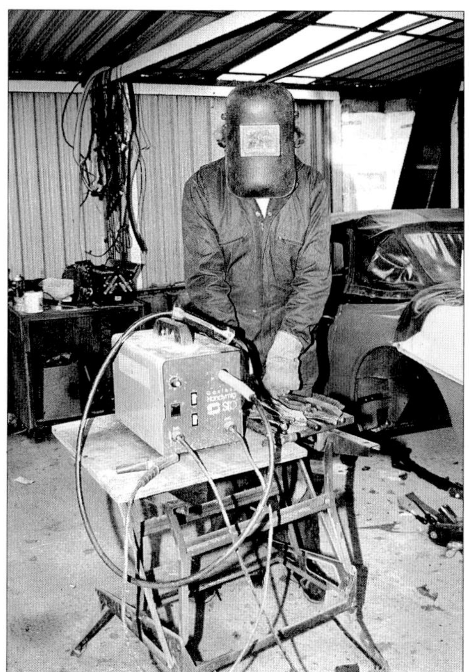

A Belt 'n braces bee-keeper? A worker in a nuclear power plant? Nope – it's me dressed up for a session of Mig welding. When welding, you should wear thick clothing to prevent splatter from burning into your skin (this HURTS!), leather gauntlets, stout shoes and, of course, a welding mask. In high summer, you'll lose pounds in weight, so be sure to drink plenty of water.

average oil-covered engine look even worse, as it does the radiator and so on. So you clean and paint or swap these components. The new paint has the same effect on the bonnet and wings, so you spray them so that their condition and colour matches that of the engine bay. Then the doors look bad against the shiny wings, then the rear quarter panels look bad viewed next to the doors …

Every part of the car which you work on will show up other areas which require attention because they look shabby in comparison. Most part-restorations grow into full restorations. Most DIY full restorations take years.

Restore cars if you think you'll enjoy restoration – if all you want is a shiny restored car, go out and buy one. You'll definitely save time and money – you'll probably save yourself a lot of heartache and possible personal injury, to boot.

SURVIVING RESTORERS

Unlike classic sports cars such as the Jaguar, Triumph and MG ranges, the Mini has not until recently attracted many specialist restorers. It was not that there weren't many Minis around at the time – there were. It was not that Mini enthusiasts did not wish to have their cars restored – they did. One problem was that few restoration professionals appreciated just how many enthusiast owners of classic Minis there were and, as a result, the restoration trade tended to underestimate the potential offered by the Mini. Another consideration is the fact that there are an awful lot of Minis on the roads, and many of the more elderly examples were treated as jalopies and allowed to quietly deteriorate to beyond the point of economic restoration. Also on the subject of economics, a good, professionally restored Mini is unlikely to attract a value greater than a fraction of its restoration costs and few people as a consequence commission top-quality professional restorations – another reason for the dearth of specialised Mini restorers.

Happily, not only is the number of Mini restorers growing today, but those restorers have the means to advertise their presence in the growing number of club magazines and classic car magazines and, of course, *Mini World*. Finding the right restorer for your Mini, however, is still far from easy.

There are many conscientious individuals and businesses employed in automotive mechanical repair and in restoration. There are also some people best avoided. The motor trade has something of a bad reputation but in reality it is just a microcosm of society in general – saints and sinners are to be found in both. However, to the inexpert, the whole car repair and restoration trade can be a jungle in which survival can be a matter of luck – he can be fortunate and deal with an honest and scrupulous business, or unlucky and in his innocence deal with a villain. Without knowledge of the 'secret arts' of elementary spannering, for instance, he can be robbed by a crooked mechanic even during a simple 6-month service through work being charged for but not done, components listed on the bill but not fitted. With restoration the amount of money at stake – and with it the risks – rise.

Nobody likes an 'armchair expert', but having some knowledge of what maintenance and repair work entails can be the very best safeguard against being cheated if you have your car maintained or repaired professionally. In exactly the same way, the secret to surviving professional restorers is knowing a lot about the subject of restoration, even if you don't possess the actual skills to carry out a restoration or even to change a spark plug yourself.

Before you start contacting restorers you should know enough about restoration to be able to carry out an assessment of the car yourself and compile the list of jobs which in your opinion need to be done. If you were silly enough to go to a crooked restorer without firstly doing this homework, you would be at his mercy – he could lead you as a lamb to the slaughter and charge you for work which was unnecessary, and some (for which you would be charged) which was neither necessary nor actually carried out. You might find on examining the estimate that there is no mention of a body pressing which you know to be in need of replacement – for instance, a heelboard or heelboard end repair panel – which tells you that it is the restorer's intention to patch repair or bodge this – wholly unacceptable practice.

The first step in finding a good restorer is to seek out both satisfied and dissatisfied owners of restored Minis; you can find plenty of these at your local Mini club branch, and even more at any of the major classic car shows. People who feel that their car's restorer did a good job will be keen to show the cars off – people who feel in any way cheated will be even more keen to publicise their views! The advantage of consulting local people is that they will be able to recommend (or warn you off) local restoration companies. But don't take their word for it (an enthusiastic 'recommender' could be the restorer's brother-in-law); examine their cars in minute detail, looking for rippling of body panels (shoddy finishing of areas covered with body filler or distortion during welding), door fit and, if the owners will permit, lift the door surround trim, count the thicknesses of steel at the sill top and the welding method used to join them – if there are other than two thicknesses then the extras are the remains of rotted former sill panels which, in the worst cases, could simply have been hammered inwards to be covered by a new outer sill (which will rot very quickly from the inside out).

If the sill top seam is Mig or gas welded then the restorer is not so well equipped as to possess a spot welder, not a terribly professional approach. Use a magnet to reveal any holes bridged with GRP or really deep dents full of bodyfiller. Look for this especially in the roof pillars and roof – it being common practice to thus smarten up a Mini which has been rolled onto its roof (and which is probably therefore bent and as a result practically worthless). If you suspect that a Mini has been rolled and that deep dents in the roof have been plastered-over with GRP and/or filler, feel through the roof lining for a tell-tale lump.

Don't be guided purely by how smart a car looks. The author has known of some really tidy-looking 'restored' Minis which turned out on closer inspection to represent the very pinnacle of the bodger's art and which, within three to at most five years, usually either have to be re-bodged (more filler and/or GRP, more patches welded on) or restored properly when they fail the MOT due to bodywork weakness. A full guide to appraising Minis is given in the book *Mini Restoration/Preparation/Maintenance* published by Osprey.

When you have established a short list of restorers, arrange to visit them so that they can draw up an estimate for the job and so that you can have a look at their operations. It is no bad thing to arrive a little earlier than the appointed time so that you see the workshop in its usual state rather than after it has been tidied up (and that huge tin of bodyfiller safely hidden out of sight) just to impress you. As the restorer circles your Mini – shaking his head in mock disbelief, sucking air between his teeth and furiously scribbling columns of figures onto the back of a cigarette packet – take a good look around the premises.

Appearances are important, and you must be guided by your gut reactions to what you see. If you don't feel entirely at ease with the business, boss, employees or premises then don't deal with that restorer – even if you cannot identify the exact cause of your misgivings.

A good restoration workshop will possess the following. Minis – and no other models – undergoing restoration. A Mini-owning boss and preferably Mini-enthusiast staff. Plenty of room and light, and a water-tight roof. Good quality tools neatly and methodically stored away so that they can quickly be found when needed. Spot, MiG and gas welding equipment. A pit or preferably a car lift. Staff who don't smoke in the workshop and who use appropriate safety equipment, such as gauntlets and eye protection. Combustible materials stored safely away in an outside building. The very best businesses will also have a spares sales division, and hence a good range of spares on site, all bought in at trade prices (and some of the savings passed on to the restoration customer).

A bad restoration workshop will house the following. A variety of jalopies in various states of decay or part-restored/plastered with bodyfiller in and around the workshop. Cramped working conditions, poor lighting and a leaking roof. Poor quality tools strewn about the floor so that the staff waste hours looking for the right tool if they don't trip over it first! Only gas welding equipment. Surly or over-frivolous staff whose cigarette ends lie where they fall on the floor. Tins of thinners stored next to gas heaters. 'Jumbo-sized' tubs of bodyfiller.

All restorers of monocoque cars these days should possess a spot welder and either some MiG or Tig welding equipment. If all you see around is gas welding gear, then this is not a good recommendation.

Paint spraying should never be undertaken in a general body shop or workshop, because the air is almost always full of particles of bodyfiller and other dust, silicones and other contaminating particles which make it difficult, if not impossible, to achieve good results. If a separate paint booth is not to be seen on site, the better restorer will sub-contract this part of the restoration to someone with the proper facilities. Ask.

Look at the cars being worked on. Your armchair expertise on restoration might not allow you to restore cars yourself but at least you should be able to recognise good and bad practices when you see them. For instance, check whether all rotten steel is cut out before new steel is welded in; whether new panels such as external sill panels are welded on top of hammered-in existing ones (these are both very common and very poor practice). Assess how well bodyshells are supported for major welded repairs to structural members. Check that rust-resisting measures are routinely practised such as coating seams which are to be welded with zinc paint and using seam sealer on them afterwards. A few eminently avoidable restorers have been known to deliberately ignore rust-retarding techniques and practices, simply because this helps generate future bodywork repair business for them – be warned.

Most professional restorers nowadays use body filler in moderation and, in fact, there is absolutely nothing wrong with this because, correctly used on strong, clean and rust-free steel in no more than a thin skim, bodyfiller will probably outlast the panels to which it is applied. If you see a five litre tub of the stuff in the premises of a restorer who only works on one car at a time, however, then it is difficult not to conclude that he uses huge dollops of filler to mask shoddy workmanship. GRP repair materials are another matter; these are used to bridge holes which should – on a car which is being restored – be welded (whereas body filler should only be used to build up the surface in shallow dents). If you see GRP repair kits or materials lying around (and unless the business restores GRP bodied cars like the Scimitar and TVRs) walk away.

In practice, tubs of body filler, GRP repair materials and piles of filler dust on the floor all have a habit of disappearing as if by magic when a visit from a prospective customer is envisaged.

Attitudes are equally important. The boss should not try too hard to appear to be your special buddy or hint at deals involving tax-free cash payment and the like (never, ever fall for this old trick – if you enter into a 'VAT free' deal, you will have broken the law and consequently will have no comeback on the restorer if the work falls short of your requirements), should not be condescending nor try to impress you with jargon, but should simply be pleasant, business-like and give the impression of efficiency.

The staff should be friendly enough to exchange pleasantries with you but not so chatty that they are distracted from their work by engaging you in long conversations – in other words, skiving, swinging the lead – because the owner of the car currently being restored will in effect be paying for the staff to thus entertain you, and you will similarly have to pay them to chat to other droppers-by if they restore your car. Generally, you should trust your instincts and, if you feel in any way uncomfortable in any way with the business, the staff or the premises then it's best to look elsewhere.

Ask whether you would be welcome to drop in occasionally during the restoration – if not, it's because there is likely to be something in the workshop that is not for your eyes, such as the Boss's wife's car being serviced in workshop time you are paying for, or a rusted panel on your car being hammered inwards before a cover plate is welded on top.

Insist on a full photographic record being kept of the restoration. This not only proves to you that the work you are being charged for gets done, it is a record of the work which you can show to any potential buyer in the future if, for some unfathomable reason, you should ever decide to sell your Mini. If a restorer refuses this request or tries to put you off the idea by telling you that it will add big money to the bill, walk away, because the restorer has something to hide. Ask to see photographs of previous restorations, too. In these days of cheap, quick turn-around, high street colour film processing, there is no excuse for any restorer not to keep full photographic records of all his work.

It is as well to obtain three or more estimates if possible, so that you have a basis for comparison. An estimate is just that – a supposedly educated guess of the cost of the restoration – but some restorers manipulate the estimate – massage the figures – for a variety of reasons. Very high or very low estimates should be treated with caution – there could be a plausible explanation, but the chances are that the restorer is either 'trying it on' to see whether you are daft enough to pay silly money or, conversely, is under-estimating to try and secure your business – in the which case, the final bill will (surprise!) exceed the estimate by a wide margin. The estimate should list all necessary work, all components and materials, and show labour charges and hours. A competent and well-run business will furnish a comprehensive estimate; if all you get is a vague set of figures scribbled on a scrap of paper then expect standards of workmanship to be similarly slipshod.

The most up-market restorers have superbly equipped workshops and hourly labour charges which reflect their high overheads; at the other end of the scale, some operate out of low-cost premises and lack expensive equipment, and should consequently have much lower hourly labour charges. The latter type of business might at first sight appear to be the cheaper option, but the better equipped business should be able to complete the work in a much shorter time, so that the total labour charge can be lower. In either case, always remember that a restoration company which specialises in Minis will take less time to complete the work than a non-specialist – however good.

It is always a good idea to show estimates to fellow enthusiasts, who might spot some discrepancy which has evaded your attention. For instance, the perceptive enthusiast might note that the restorer intends to weld a repair plate (which might appear on the estimate only as a part number) onto the rear subframe which – in a full restoration – is a ludicrous piece of penny-pinching.

Remember that there are many permutations of price and job specifications; these can usually be juggled to a compromise which suits your own pocket and aspirations. If the estimate is 'modular' – that is, each component of the job is costed separately – then you can select which jobs you feel confident you can do yourself, and which you would rather entrust to the professional.

Expect to have to pay a deposit on commissioning the work, and in some cases 'stage' payments as the job progresses. These payments should not come to more than the components and consumables which have to be bought in at the time the payment becomes due.

Ensure that your car will be fully insured against accidental damage while on the restorer's premises, and also that you have cover should the car be stolen or returned to you in an unacceptable or unsafe state. Use an insurance broker who specialises in the classic car market, and check the terms and conditions of your policy before taking the car to your chosen restorer. The restorer should also be insured, and if he cannot show you proof of insurance cover then go elsewhere.

Good restorers are always in demand; their workshops are always booked up for weeks or in some cases even months in advance. Don't be impressed if the restorer can start work on your Mini the following week, unless there is some indication that this is due to a cancelled restoration.

It is, of course, during the actual restoration that relations between you and the restorer can become most strained. There exists a fine line which separates taking an active interest in the restoration and being a nuisance, and another which separates keeping the Boss on his or her toes and annoying them sufficiently to incite them to drag their heels or do something nasty to your car – cross them at your peril.

Disputes between you and the restorer should be settled amicably and quickly: if a dispute cannot be settled during a friendly discussion, you're in trouble. You have all the power of modern consumer law on your side; the restorer has your car and a cutting torch, so tread very carefully.

SURVIVING DIY RESTORATION

Few first-time restorers realise just how much work they are letting themselves in for; some restorations take months, some years and a large percentage are never finished at all. One of my neighbours started restoring a Mini back in 1990 – it is still not completed as this is being written five years later.

A lot of heartache could be avoided by starting off with a realistic appraisal of the spare time and facilities at your disposal, your skills and most especially your dogged determination to see the job through.

Never under-estimate just how great an undertaking a full Mini restoration really is. Removing the engine is hard work in itself, but before you can get to work on that bodywork there are still plenty of components yet to be removed.

The Full Works. Stripping the car down to a bare shell means that you can weld fairly confident that the shell will not catch fire! However, beware small inflammable objects such as foam rubber which may be jammed into small crevices.

How well do you cope with seemingly insurmountable problems? If you are the kind of person who is likely to suffer deep dejection when the paint topcoat blisters or the clutch master cylinder leaks fluid onto your shiny new paintwork, then perhaps you are not really suited to restoration. You have to be pessimistic so that setbacks don't come as a surprise, phlegmatic enough to shrug your shoulders and get on with dealing with setbacks without hysterics. A degree of optimism keeps you going through bad patches. You need a passionate desire to get the restoration finished, as many end up in limbo with the falling away of motivation. A talent for self-deception helps because it allows you to convince yourself that things are better than they really are. But you have to be a realist, able to recognise when you are out of your depth, when to walk away from the workshop because if you stay, you are going to cause more problems than you cure. There you have it. The ideal amateur restorer is a pessimistic optimist, an excitable stoic, and a self-deceiving realist.

Before committing yourself to a restoration, why not try a 'toe in the water'; exercise to see whether it's for you? Seek out another enthusiast locally who is restoring a car and offer your assistance. This will give you first-hand experience of what's involved so that you can decide whether you are really the type to last a DIY restoration – at no cost to yourself.

Then consider the financial aspect of the restoration. Carry out an appraisal of the car; bodywork, mechanical components and trim. Cost the exercise out, not forgetting to account for paint, welding consumables, electricity and so on. Look at the total projected cost and consider whether it might be better to sell your own car and buy a ready-restored one instead. It usually is.

Few first-time restorers appreciate just how expensive a DIY restoration can be; in 1994 at the time of writing it is – believe it or not – possible to approach five-figure sums on Mini repair panels plus mechanical and electrical components during the restoration (or, more properly, the complete reconstruction) of a really poor example. If you wish to rebuild a car to as-new condition then unfortunately you're going to have to shell out as much as you would have to in order to buy a new Mini at today's prices.

The only way to bring costs substantially down is to clean and re-use tired components instead of acquiring exchange reconditioned or newly-manufactured ones. This is fine for a car which is to receive light and occasional use, but for a car which is to be relied upon for daily transport it is folly.

The next question is where to obtain spares? In my experience, some Mini spares specialists are better than other types of supplier not least because they are staffed by very knowledgeable Mini enthusiasts – other suppliers have staff whose lack of specialised Mini knowledge, not to mention lack of enthusiasm, can result in them selling you the 'wrong' spare for the year of your Mini. The best spares suppliers all tend to incorporate workshop and sometimes full restoration facilities, so that the staff are in an environment which gives them a good all-round working knowledge of the car as well as access to the knowledge of the workshop staff.

Even so, one of the very best investments the Mini owner can make is a manufacturer's parts catalogue, which gives the correct code number for each and every spare. Guided by this, there should really be no room for misunderstanding on either part.

RESTORATION VS RECONSTRUCTION

There is an important distinction to be made between restoring a Mini and reconstructing it. Restoration is really 'renovation', because it involves stripping components from the car, repairing, rebuilding and repainting them – in other words, renovating them. Mini owners enjoy easy access to new and reconditioned spares, and can take the easier (but more expensive) route of simply buying new or exchange reconditioned components. This process is actually reconstruction rather than restoration, and the greater the emphasis on reconstruction in a restoration the higher the eventual cost.

Of course, the great overhead in renovation is the time requirement, and the trade-off is thus our time and effort versus our money. For example: a car has a leaking brake wheel cylinder, due to a damaged seal. The renovator acquires a seal kit, spends maybe two hours removing, disassembling, cleaning and honing the cylinder before fitting the new seals. The reconstructer unbolts his backplate assemblies complete and exchanges them for reconditioned ones, in the process, spending many times as much money as the renovator but doing the job in a fraction of the time.

Most car restorations are a mixture of renovation and reconstruction, with the accent on reconstruction in the case of the Mini because the car is so well served with quality spares.

DIY restoration – even in cases where the accent is on renovation – is most certainly not a cheap route to ownership of a nice Mini. In addition to the costs of the actual restoration, most people have to invest quite large sums in the large range of tools which will be needed. Before even that overhead can be taken into consideration, there comes the problem of premises.

PREMISES

Minis have been restored in the open in gardens and in polythene-covered lean-tos, but few people will be able to produce their best work in such unwelcoming environments for the course of a full restoration (which usually incorporates at least one winter). What you need is a proper workshop.

Wooden buildings have a lot going for them – in particular the sound and heat insulation qualities of wood. Furthermore, the workshop should not suffer from condensation dripping from the roof and down the walls – the greatest drawback of steel buildings; against building in wood is the obvious fire hazard. It's bad enough having a car full of inflammable materials and such potentially explosive substances as petrol, thinners and the like in a workshop without also having an inflammable workshop! The alternatives are steel cladding or bricks and mortar. Get into brick with a proper tiled pitched roof if possible – with steel cladding, condensation in winter can be a real problem and, on hot summer mornings, steel-clad buildings rapidly turn into ovens. As an absolute minimum, the work area should be large enough to accommodate two cars – and preferably three – in order to give sufficient space to restore one.

TOOLS

The tools needed for restoration are not cheap but it is advisable to buy the very best quality you can afford, because cheap tools usually break just as you really need them – and when

Mig welding machines don't cost a lot nowadays. I opted for the gasless Sip, because it means I've just one consumable – the cored wire – to run out of.

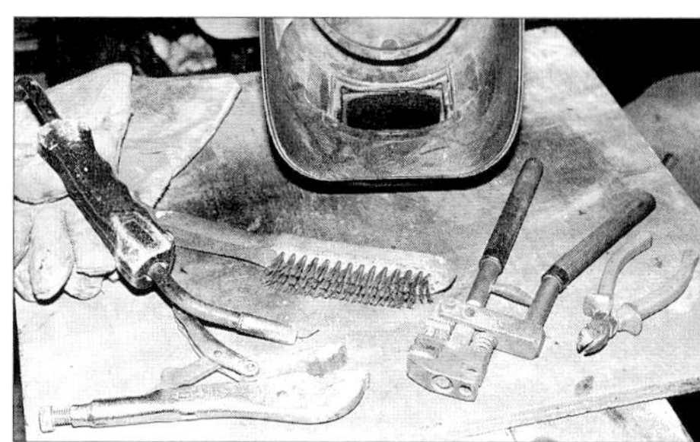

In addition to a welder, you need a mask (I recommend the wrap-around type) plus gauntlets. A wire brush and joddler also come in handy.

You can buy sets of hammer and dollies at fairly low cost, but if you cannot afford a full set, it's surprising what can be achieved with nothing more complicated than a small hammer plus sundry pieces of wood to act as dollies.

tools break they often damage the components or fittings on which they are being used. However, good quality tools (apart from those which fall off the backs of lorries) are for many, prohibitively expensive. If so, buy a cheap set of spanners initially, but replace those which wear out (which receive the highest use) with better quality alternatives. If you do this, you'll probably find that the 7/16 in., 1/2 in. and 9/16 in. spanners get the highest usage and hence wear out first. The same replacement system applies to sockets.

Buy the best in components and consumables. For example, you can find reconditioned exchange gearboxes and engines offered by back-street companies at very low prices, but it is always better to buy from a recognised specialist supplier and to pay the higher price which they will charge. It is far from unknown for some cheap 'reconditioned' engines to turn out to have merely been cleaned and painted! Cheap paint and thinners will not only jeopardise the paint finish, but will usually be more difficult to work with than good quality stuff.

MENTAL ATTITUDE

In survivalist terms, restoring a car is roughly equivalent to making it to the South Pole on a pogo stick. DIY restoration can be hell.

It's all down to your state of mind. If things are going well then you're bound to be in a good state of mind, but the reason things go well is simply *because* you're in a good state of mind – not the other way around. Consider the opposite scenario; you're feeling depressed, angry or just plain old mentally tired. Your mind is not really on the job and the spanner slips off the nut or the stud shears so that your hand smashes into one of the many and varied sharp objects cunningly placed for this very purpose on the car.

State of mind is similarly capable of causing MiG welders to burn through expensive body panels, fresh paint on a perfectly prepared surface to blister and chrome trim to buckle as you're struggling to fit it onto the car. Few restorations progress without serious setbacks, most commonly the discovery of former butchery or bodgery – welded patches either end of the heelboard, huge lumps of bodyfiller plastered into chicken wire stretched across a gaping hole – that sort of thing. Be warned, there will be situations which can see your mood fluctuating between suicidal and homicidal: I know – I've been there.

When your spirits hit rock bottom, the only sensible solution is to lock up the workshop and walk away. Do something completely different; something which you enjoy doing and which you're good at. Do something which cheers you up, and do it for long enough to erase the recent memory of problems with the restoration.

Prevention is always better than cure; there are ways in which you can mentally prepare yourself for what could otherwise be disastrous sessions in the workshop. List the jobs you intend to do then sit down and think them through: having a list of jobs means that you don't end up wandering aimlessly around the workshop wondering what to do next, or try to tackle jobs in the wrong order.

Perhaps the workshop could be made more comfortable. Install a radio and tune it to a station which broadcasts relaxing music (I find the classics are best, but this is of course a personal choice) – not to pointless chat shows which can distract you and which can draw you into taking sides in the discussion or argument and getting distacted unnecessarily. Plaster the walls with prints of Minis, to remind you of what you car will hopefully look like when it's completed. Install a chair, so that you can sit down and relax when you have to think some problem through.

Try to become more organised in your work; keep a list of tools, spares and consumables which will be needed and regularly update this so that you aren't prevented from working for want of a gasket set or a roll of Mig wire. If any job starts to bore or frustrate you, leave it and move on to another job which is more interesting or straightforward before you grind to a halt or begin to make silly mistakes – when you come back to the original job it will usually prove much easier.

You will see much faster progress from a number of short work sessions than from the same amount of time in a single session. Seven two-hour work periods a week are generally preferable to two seven-hour periods at weekends. End each session in the workshop by tidying up, so that all of your tools are in their correct places and cleaned of grease ready for the next time.

Visitors to your workshop can be a blessing or a bane: only invite fellow DIY (or professional) restorers *and keep all sightseers at bay.* Lock them out if necessary, because they'll not only distract you with countless pointless questions, the answers to which are of no benefit to them and are instantly forgotten, but they are prone to lean on freshly painted bodywork, to tread on repair panels, to smear their greasy paws all over panels which are prepared for painting and kick over tins of paint.

A visit from a fellow restorer, on the other hand, is most likely to inject new enthusiasm into the project, especially if the visitor rolls his or (occasionally) her sleeves up and joins in the fun. It's always more enjoyable working on someone else's car and, when you suddenly find an enthusiastic volunteer helping in the Good Work, you'll want to work as well. Two people work three times as fast as one.

Never be afraid to bite the bullet and call in professional assistance. It would, for instance, work out cheaper in the long run to have sills welded up professionally than it would to attempt the work yourself and have to replace the lot if your welding proves anything less than 100% sound! Similarly, it can prove less expensive to have the paint preparation and spraying carried out professionally than to have to buy a decent compressor, oil/water filter and spraygun, not to mention two or more lots of paint if things go wrong – and be warned that things often go wrong when amateurs point a spray gun at a car!

Although many of the people who claim to have fully restored their cars have actually brought in professionals to do much (in many cases, most) of the work and are happy to bask in the reflected glory of the professional's work, there is no shame in admitting such involvement and certainly no glory in attempting tasks beyond your abilities and making a mess of things. Your life could depend on the quality of the welding, in the integrity of the wiring, the efficiency of the braking system – once the car is out on the roads. Don't risk it – summon professional help whenever you feel the slightest bit out of your depth.

To be brutally frank, far from feeling admiration for the genuine 100% DIY restorer, you should pity him. His is a particularly moving type of madness, as you'll see from the following description of a typical restoration.

STRIPDOWN

Despite being faced with problems like seized nuts, bolts and self-tapping screws, stripping the car down to a bare shell is a comparatively easy part of the restoration as a whole, and there is a great temptation to rush this – in the process, losing track of where components are stored and even forgetting where (and which way up) some of them fit on the car! Far better to take your time and clean everything which comes off the car, catalogue and store spares in a logical order so that that they can be found again.

I strongly recommend that you take time to photograph every part of the car before stripping away components, to act as an aid to memory when the time comes to re-fit them. It is surprisingly easy to forget where some small bracket fits, or which precise route a cable or length of brake pipe should follow – I speak on this subject from personal experience. If you

Whether to carry out rebuilds of the engine and 'box, buy ready-reconditioned units or salvage something from the scrapyard and keep your fingers crossed that it is serviceable is by no means an easy decision. If your budget is tight then the breaker's is usually the cheapest alternative; if money is no object go for professionally reconditioned units. Don't be deceived into thinking that a DIY reconditioning will necessarily be cheaper than a pro-recon – it might cost far more, depending on the condition of the units and the amount of work.

Unless you sincerely want a lifetime doomed to excruciating back pain, never try to lift the Mini engine/gearbox. Use lifting gear – and not one of those little ratchet winches which the small print on the packet thoughtfully explains are for horizontal pulling and not for vertical lifting.

Gearboxes are a problem. If you renew any of the gears to cure a noise, they won't mesh too well with the laygear – so you'll have to replace the laygear – which won't mesh well with the other gears, and you can end up replacing the lot – and that costs a fortune! Better to go for a reconditioned unit.

Mini flywheels usually pop off with the least encouragement. Usually. This intransigent little devil cost me two days fruitless slog before it came away. Had the engine been in the car, I'd still be wrestling with it today! Moral – renew the clutch while the engine is out.

A restoration gives you the opportunity to attend to every single component if wished, cleaning dirt from the carburettor fuel bowl can prevent that dirt causing problems with the float valve leading to engine flooding.

If the callipers on your project car look anything like this, budget for replacement rather than repair.

have colour photographs there should be no such problems.

Store those components which are to be re-used in dry conditions, because the time interval between stripping and rebuilding can turn out to be many times longer than your initial

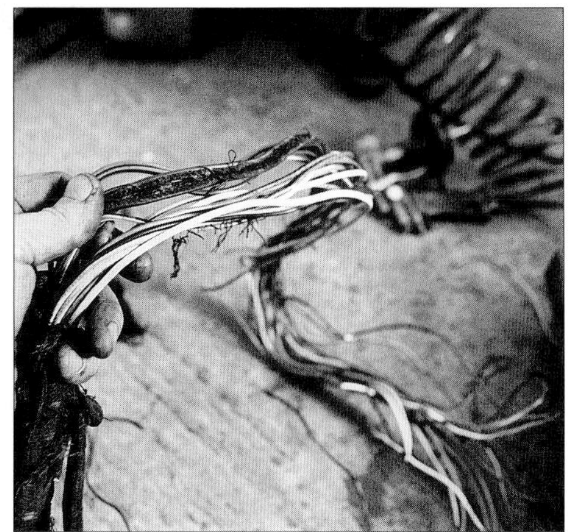

If you renew the loom, never throw the old loom away. The wires and connectors can all come in handy.

estimate and there's little more depressing than finding the next component to be re-fitted has rusted to the point of being useless.

Keep small items such as nuts and bolts in freezer bags, which can be sealed to keep out moisture and which have a panel on which you can write a description of the components inside. Any non-metal components (any leather, plastics, vinyl) should be kept safe from rodent attack!

It is worthwhile slowing down the stripdown process and taking the time to separate the components into three groups. The first contains items which, with no more than cleaning, can be re-used, the second those on which some DIY reconditioning work is needed and the third comprises items which will have to be replaced.

Working slowly and methodically, taking time to sort and catalogue spares and photographing everything might at first sight appear to be unnecessarily time-consuming but, unless you are fully acquainted with the mechanical, electrical, trim and hydraulic components of the Mini, the extra time you spend working in this way now can save you far more time later on when you come to rebuild the car!

BODYWORK

Contrary to the opinions of some commentators, obtaining consistently strong and neat MiG welds is not easy, and if anyone tells you that it is easy, the only explanation is that they have no personal experience of the process and are merely reiterating what they have been told by another armchair expert or have read somewhere. Comparatively few DIY restorers appear to carry out welded repairs to their own cars, sensibly bringing in a mobile welder.

As with painting, the application of the weld or paint takes little time in comparison with that needed for preparation. You could, for instance, spend a month or more cutting out rot, cleaning edges (which are to be welded) back to bright steel, tailoring repair panels and preparing them for welding, and then bring in a mobile welder who can weld the lot up in a few hours. I was once taken to task by a classic car club technical adviser for recommending bringing in a mobile welder on the basis that these mobile welders were all self-taught cowboys. In fact, if you look in your local trade telephone directory you'll find that the majority of advertisements for mobile welders will state their qualifications; there are cowboys out there but they are in the minority and – if you insist on seeing credentials – easily avoided.

A mobile welder will charge by the hour, and perhaps have a standing 'call-out' charge. The hourly labour rate should be a fraction of that charged by a restoration company to carry out the same work on its own premises, and so great savings are possible by adopting this semi-DIY restoration method.

The most important aspect of structural bodywork repair is to ensure that the bodyshell is not in the least distorted before new metal is welded on. Obvious though that may appear, it is far from unknown for restored Minis to 'crab' when underway because the bodyshell was not correctly supported when the sills were welded on! In the absence of a jig, you have to

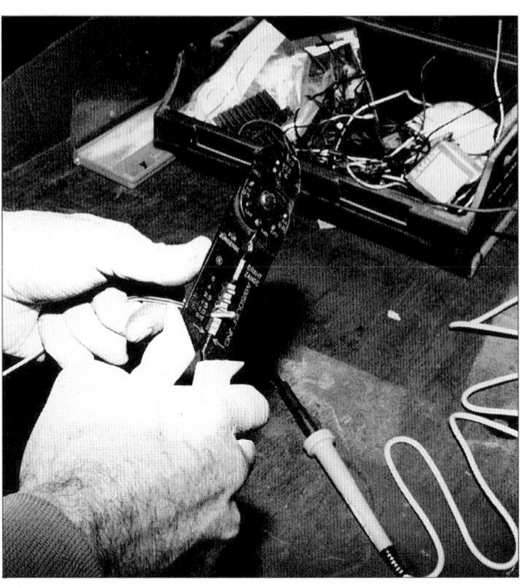

The modern way of joining wires is to use crimping connectors, but a soldered joint is, in my opinion, preferable. Place a length of heat-shrink tube on one of the wires, then strip the ends of the wires and twist them together.

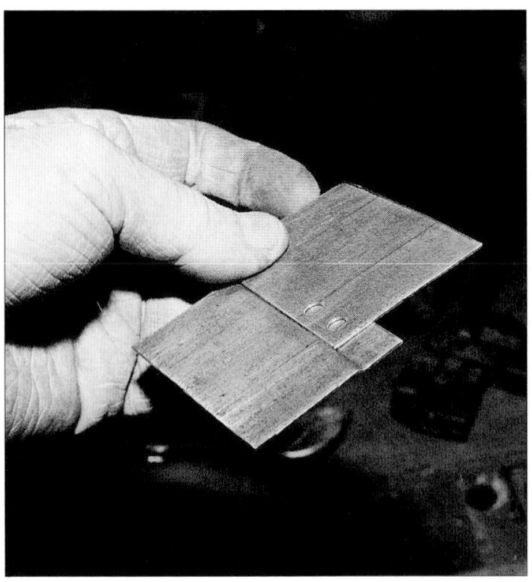

Two methods of welding. I've placed a step in the edge of the one panel, and punched two holes in the other, through which I'm going to weld – referred to as 'plug' or 'puddle' welding). I'll then seam weld the rest.

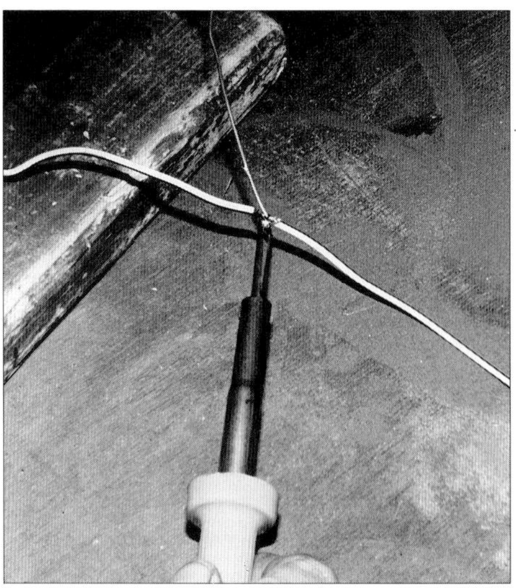

The object of soldering is to get heat into the joint, which encourages the solder to flow deep into the joint. Heat it from one side, and feed on solder wire from the other.

resort to endless measuring to ensure that dimensions are the same either side of the car and checking levels using a spirit level.

When the bodyshell *is* level, it pays to support the main structural points so solidly that nothing short of a direct hit from a field gun can shift anything. This not only guards against workshop visitors who appear incapable of supporting their own weight and always choose the weakest part of the bodyshell to lean on or sit on, but also guards against accidents – for instance, if you stumble, you tend to put your hand out instinctively to check your fall, and if the shell is in the way it can move if not properly supported.

Ideally, the front subframe – or, if this has been removed, the bottom edge of the toe board – would be supported and the main crossmember would have supports. The rear end of the central tunnel would have a flat support which spread the load and the boot floor would have its own supports. Many restorers

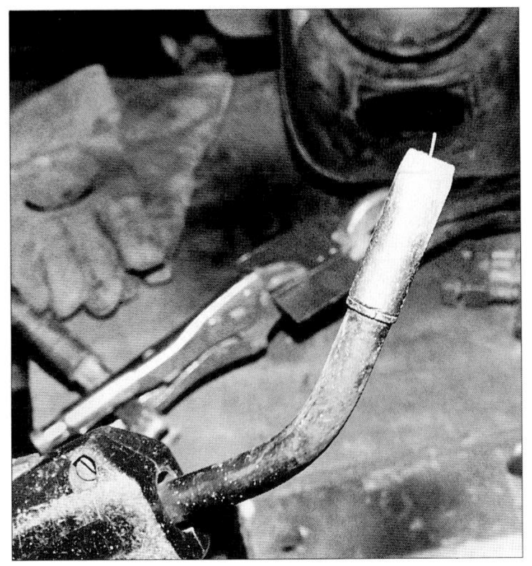

Clean the areas to be welded. Trim the wire to 10mm in length, attach the earth clamp to the work piece.

A lot of sparks fly when you weld, creating two potential hazards. The sparks will ignite any combustible materials, so make sure there are none near, and they hurt if they land on your skin so, no matter how hot the day, wear plenty of thick clothing.

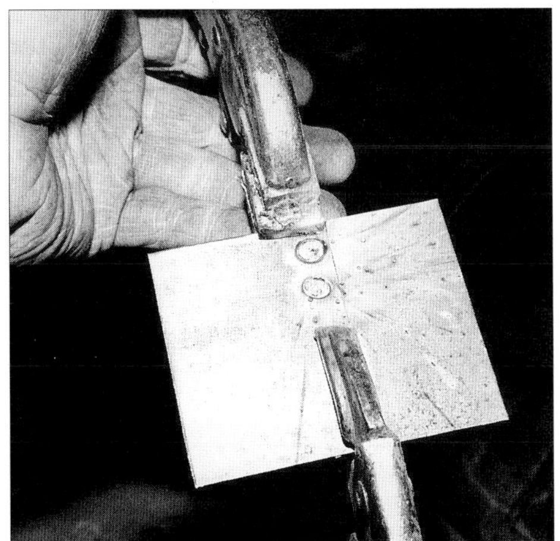

Plug welds are useful for replacing spot welds and, done carefully, there will be little or no proud weld to have to grind down. If you opt to spot weld, bear in mind that most domestic spot welders seem to have a limitation of two 1mm thick sheets of steel – insufficient for many car repair jobs.

This is the back of the welded joint. Note how well the weld has penetrated the lower sheet, giving a very strong and neat joint.

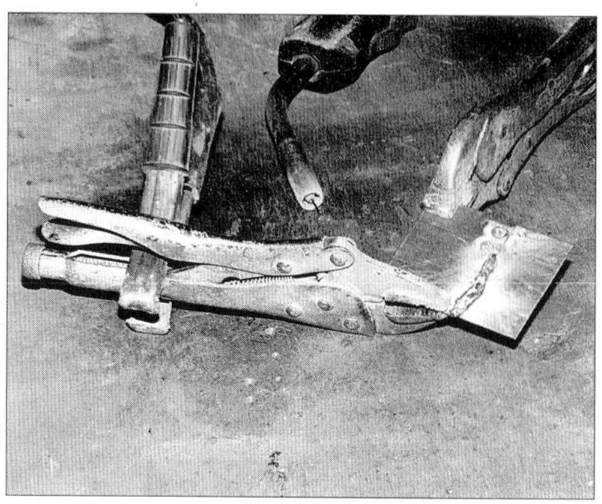

I've seam welded the rest of the joint, but had the Mig wire feed speed too high, which has produced a lot of proud weld to grind away afterwards. Had the feed speed been too low, the result would have been burning holes in the steel. Experiment on scrap steel until you discover the optimum setting for various types of joint and thickness of steel.

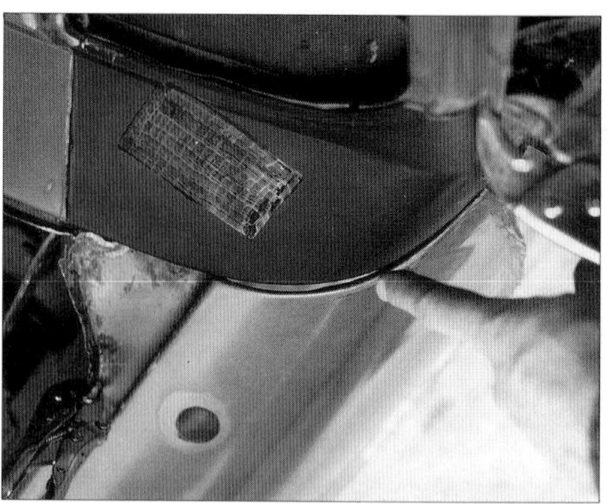

Whether you're replacing the wing, repairing the top scuttle end – or both – you might find that the two panels don't align without considerable re-shaping. This is normal, and the all-round restorer will by default acquire considerable panel beating skills to make repair panels fit.

Before you weld on a repair panel, you'll probably have to carry out some welded repair to the underlying panels. If you're working on a budget (aren't we all?) then panelwork which is out of sight can usually be fabricated at home.

This is the repair panel you'll need to make to go under the scuttle end – it's not difficult to fabricate, and is a good introduction to panel beating (more usually called 'tin bashing'!).

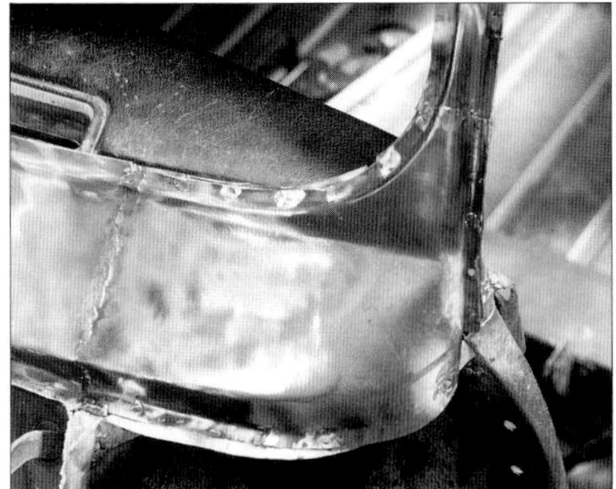

The more accurately you cut out the rot and fit the repair panel, the less bodyfiller or lead you'll need afterwards. For a tricky repair like this, try to adjust the Mig settings so that you aren't left with too much weld to have to grind down afterwards – it's awkward grinding around the pillar join.

The sill assembly with the doorstep cut away. It is not unusual to find that one or more of the sill components is a repair panel welded on top of the rotten original; cut them both out and start afresh.

With the benefit of hindsight, I now know that this is far from the best way to remove an old outer sill panel. Quite apart from the dangers of cutting myself through not wearing gloves, I could have saved myself a lot of sweat by drilling out the spot welds in the lip, then parting the joint using a chisel made from a sharpened length of industrial hacksaw blade.

Before welding on a panel which will create an enclosed area, take the opportunity to paint everything which will be covered. The masking tape is protecting the areas where the weld will be made, and these will be sprayed with zinc-based weld through primer.

Few older Minis will retain their original sills, and you may find that the quality of previous repairs falls short of exemplary. The inner edge is secured only by sparse tack welds, and the panel is not welded to the jacking point reinforcer. Please note: the only reason I'm not wearing gloves in these photographs is that I have to operate the camera – impossible when wearing welding gauntlets. You have no excuse – wear leather gloves.

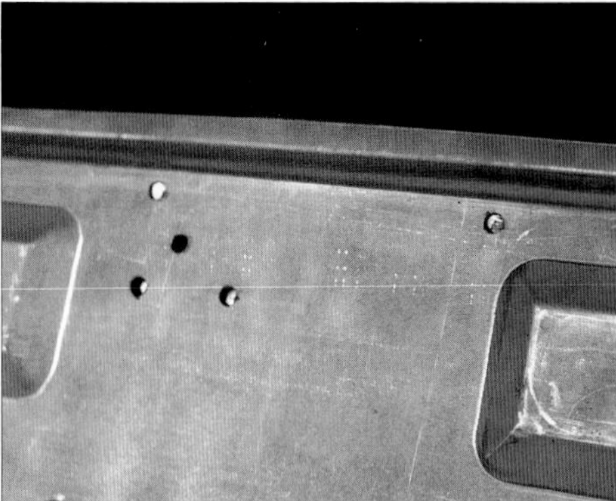

This sill repair panel had no hole for the jacking point, so I had to make my own using the drill to cut a series of holes and a file to join them up! The extra holes in this photo are for plug welding the panel onto the jacking point assembly.

Some cars might need limited welded repair; the battery box base is usually the very first area to rot and, although you can fabricate and weld in a new base, it doesn't take long to drill out the spot welds and jack the entire assembly out. In either case, this quick and easy repair is made more difficult because the fuel tank HAS to be removed; in fact, the fuel tank and lines plus the brake hydraulic lines and hoses should be removed before any welded repair.

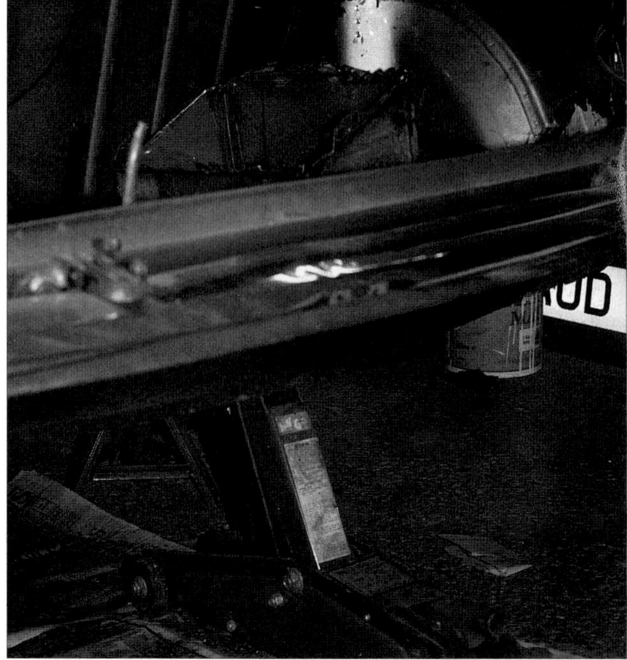

weld braces across the door apertures before cutting away rotten metal, and this is good practice.

However carefully you measure and support the bodyshell, it is essential to keep checking for both bodyshell distortion and the accuracy or otherwise of panel placement by offering adjacent panels into position – for instance, temporarily fitting the doors and the front wings to check shut lines before welding the sills to the A and B posts.

Don't assume that repair panels are necessarily accurate – many are damaged in transit and some are made that way! Get the shell straight and alter the repair panel so that it fits – NEVER the other way around!

When fitting a repair panel, don't fit the entire panel if you don't have to, but cut it down to the smallest practicable size which still allows you to weld to strong metal. Welded repair panels always rot out firstly along the welded seam, so that when you have to repeat the repair you can still use a standard repair panel rather than the full panel. For instance, if you cut down a quarter repair panel then when you have to repeat the repair in years to come you can still use a repair panel rather than a half or full wing.

Two repairs commonly found on otherwise good bodyshells. The scuttle end is very prone to rot, and the A panel is also susceptible. Before welding in panels like this, I always offer up the wings or other adjacent panels, to make sure that everything will line up.

PAINTWORK

Catastrophes seems to have a habit of occurring the instant a spray gun is pointed at a car. Even experienced professionals in well-equipped paint shops who follow the text book to the letter have occasional disasters, let alone the majority of us DIYers who operate in draughty damp sheds and whose paintwork problems are generally of our own making.

Most written works on automotive paintwork contain very little of relevance to the DIY enthusiast, but describe painting under ideal conditions in a fairytale fashion which the embittered amateur with an unfortunate wealth of empirical experience might harshly regard as glib. Read all you like on the subject but, like riding a bike, swimming or MiG welding without blasting holes in panels, the only real teacher is experience, usually bad experience.

The key to surviving car painting is recognising when to Walk Away And Leave It. Trying to rectify problems which occur during painting normally exacerbates those problems. Those who are foolish enough to spray cellulose without wearing the appropriate respiratory gear are most at risk in this respect – completely spaced-out on thinner fumes, they compound problems which, if left to their own devices, can simply disappear. Paint runs are an obvious example. If left alone to dry, lesser

I find high-volume, low pressure (HVLP) spray equipment a better prospect for the DIY restorer than the traditional small tank compressor and spray gun. It is cleaner, less wasteful of paint and easier to use.

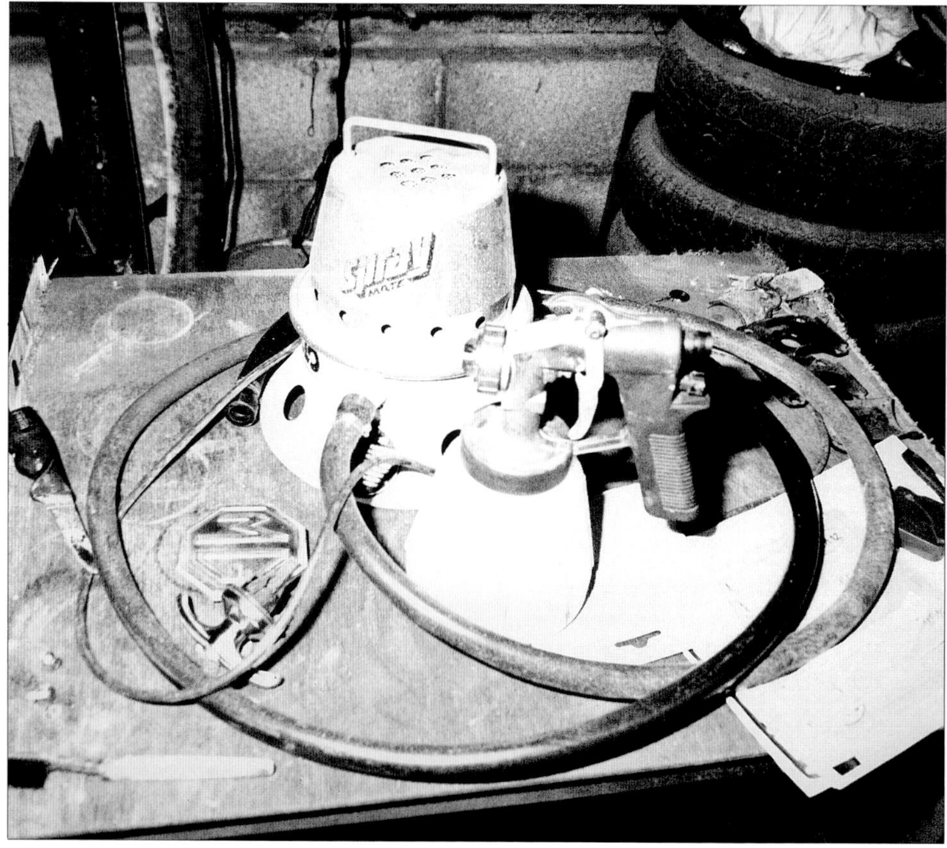

runs can disappear completely (especially if the paint is cellulose) and larger runs can quite easily be flatted out with 1000 grit wet 'n dry and the surface lightly cut after the paint has cured. Yet the amateur who finds himself gazing at a solitary run can, in trying to mop up the surplus with an artist's paintbrush or a rag, contaminate the paint or even damage the underlying coats if thinners have sufficiently softened them. Walk Away And Leave It.

The second survival hint for painting is not to be careless. A friend of the author's with a lifetime of experience of paint spraying cars once inadvertently thinned his cellulose paint with brake fluid – which had been 'temporarily' stored in an empty thinners tin. This is not a good idea, and the following day the still-tacky paint had to be stripped off and it was back to Square One. The same person sprayed a large panel on which paint stripper had been used nearly a year before, and found streaks of wet paint where traces of stripper remained – he now thoroughly washes all panels before painting them. The author has spot-primed areas and neglected to flat the surrounding area of dry spray at the edges before applying the topcoats. When this was subsequently flatted, the dry spray broke through as thousands of tiny grey spots.

Before spraying paint – whether it's primer or the final topcoat – set out everything you're going to need and check that you're using the correct paint and thinners, that the spray gun is spotlessly clean inside and out, that the surface to be painted is free of finger prints, dead insects and the like, that you have clean tack rags and clean rags for the spirit wipe. You could even usefully draw up a list of jobs to be tackled (in the correct order) and materials to be used, and pin this to the workshop wall.

SPRAYING EQUIPMENT

If you can afford to buy a reasonably large compressor with, say, a 100 litre tank, a high quality spraygun and a good oil/water trap, then all well and good. Most DIY restorers struggle with smaller compressors which are unable to supply a sufficiently high volume of compressed air to operate spray guns satisfactorily. For years, I struggled with a small compressor which could not maintain the 50psi needed to spray cellulose (which resulted in poor paint atomisation and a narrow spray fan), and which had a nasty habit of overheating and cutting out when I was part-way across a panel. Worse, the oil/water trap failed to do its job properly and, as a result, a yellow emulsion (a mixture of oil and water) would intermittently spit out of the gun – ruining the surface.

The alternative to conventional spray equipment is the High Volume Low Pressure (HVLP) system. This uses a turbine to feed a gun with a high volume of warmed, low pressure air, and it offers many significant advantages over compressor systems for DIY spraying. Firstly, it is very quiet, making no more noise than a vacuum cleaner, so you won't annoy your neighbours. Secondly, it is continually rated, and will run all day with no overheating and cutting out. Thirdly, the low pressure eliminates bounce-back which, with conventional equipment, not only fills the atmosphere with paint dust but also wastes a lot of material. There is little or no over-spray, so that masking-up takes far less time, and there is no oil/water emulsion problem. I use the Apollo 400 – the smallest of the Apollo family of HVLP spraying systems – and would recommend it to anyone. A friend who restores cars for a living recently acquired the larger Apollo 700 – and says it is the best investment his company ever made.

Irrespective of what equipment you choose, painting can still be a fraught business – insects landing on wet paint on warm days, paint blooming on cold. Air-blown debris from neighbour's bonfires, dust, leaves, silicones – everything can appear to conspire against the DIY painter. If there is one single aspect of a

DIY restoration best farmed out to professionals, it is the application of the topcoats. This is never cheap, so most DIY restorers soldier on as best they can.

And the very best of luck.

BOXING UP

The final part of a restoration is the boxing up, the re-fitting of trim and mechanical components to the bodyshell. In theory, this should be the easiest and by far the most enjoyable part of the restoration if for no other reason than because it's the Home Straight and the end of the restoration is in sight.

In practice, boxing up is rarely straightforward. New or reconditioned components may not fit because they are for the wrong year of car; soft, fresh paintwork can so easily be damaged if you are the least bit careless; electrical components might not function or the engine might refuse to start due to a fuel delivery or ignition problem if you're lucky, or something more fundamental such as an out-of-timing camshaft if you're not.

Whether you have fitted a new loom or not, electrical problems can drive you to distraction. When you come to reconnect the battery, ensure that everything is switched 'off' then attach the live terminal and momentarily touch the earth terminal to its post. If you see and hear a spark at the post then something is leaking to earth, and the battery should on no account be connected until you have traced the fault – *otherwise, you could start an electrical fire.*

You have the option of physically going over the entire wiring system trying to locate the fault visually, which is not always possible, or using a multi-meter to trace the fault. With the battery live terminal disconnected and the multi-meter set to measure resistance (the scale which registers ohms), connect one of the multi-meter terminals to earth (the bodywork) and begin tracing the fault at the fuse block. Remove each fuse and touch the other terminal of the multi-meter against each fuse mount. When you find the one which offers low resistance, use a wiring diagram to trace the individual circuits which are connected with the fuse, and check the terminals until you locate the one causing the problem. If you cannot trace the fault then bring in a mobile auto-electrician who can.

Always think two or three jobs ahead. It is unfortunately very easy to approach a sequence of tasks in such a way that you have to remove the first component which you fitted in order to be able to fit the last! Referring to your photographic record of the initial stripdown is a great aid in avoiding this.

The author prefers not to set a deadline for the rebuild, so that he works at his own pace and avoids forcing errors which might be brought about by racing against the clock; the MOT is not booked until the car is finished and fully tested – avoiding all-night fault tracing sessions which can otherwise see the restorer bleary-eyed and anything but bushy-tailed the following morning at the MOT testing station.

But when you have restored a Mini and are rewarded for your efforts with an MOT certificate, you will feel a sense of satisfaction which few achieve.

If you suspect that your funds are about to run too low to be able to finish the restoration, try to concentrate your spending on the essentials rather than the cosmetics. Get the braking system 100% sound rather than blow the money on a shiny new rear bumper! If money is tight, leave ordering expensive items of trim until last, so that all of your available funds go into the important areas. Unfortunately, not everyone gets their priorities right in this respect and, as a result, there are a great many beautiful looking but less than roadworthy restored cars around.

If, like so many people, your funds do run out before the car is roadworthy, spend your last few quid on a dustsheet and laid-up insurance. As already shown, a part-completed restoration project car is not valued according to the work that has gone into it in the market; but, if you are prepared to put the project on hold until funds permit its completion, you will eventually end up with a valuable asset.

PRO-AM RESTORATIONS

Relatively few full restorations can claim to be wholly 'DIY'; most include some element of professional assistance. Leaving aside the vanity which leads people to claim to have personally carried out restorations when in fact quite often the bulk of the work was contracted out, this is for the majority the most sensible route to a sound and roadworthy restored car.

We have already established that the bulk of the work in a restoration is unskilled cleaning and scraping – the sort of work anyone can do and something only the rich will hand over to an over-qualified professional restorer at big bucks per hour! It is, however, worth paying the going rate to have the relatively small amount of highly skilled work in a restoration carried out professionally.

The most common pro-am restoration sees the initial stripdown being undertaken at home, the bare bodyshell being delivered to a restorer for welded repairs and spraying, then the car being reconstructed (using new or reconditioned components) at home afterwards. You should be rewarded with a substantial reduction in the bill, but you must be warned that the chances are you'll seriously underestimate both the amount of work you are letting yourself in for and the length of time the build-up will take. Differences of opinion between you and the restorer are quite likely to arise if, for instance, you discover a scratch in the paintwork which you are sure is not of your making and which the restorer accepts no liability for.

A cheaper form of pro-am restoration is for you to strip down the car but to contract out various parts of the restoration to specialist companies to complete on their own premises – one for welded repair, another for paintwork (you can save a small fortune by doing the paint prep. yourself), and finally another for the build-up. Although the vast bulk of the restoration is carried out by professionals, you should achieve a worthwhile overall saving by virtue of the fact that you can select the most appropriate (fastest) company for each individual aspect of the restoration. The problem with this form of 'managed' restoration is that each specialist will blame the other if anything goes wrong, and it can prove nigh-on impossible to pin the blame on any of them.

The most cost-effective pro-am restoration which brings the greatest savings of all is to keep the car at your home throughout and to bring mobile specialists in to carry out the various jobs on your premises – with the obvious exception of painting. The benefits are that you get a top-quality professional job at the lowest price, that you remain in full charge throughout, and that you yourself only carry out those jobs with which you're entirely comfortable. The negative aspect is that the restoration can easily turn into a full-time occupation for you – and you'll be working for no wages!

Chapter Four

Surviving Breakdowns

With the sole exception of the recent fuel injected Minis (by virtue of same), the simplicity of the Mini helps make it an especially reliable car well into its dotage, and properly maintained examples – regardless of age or variant – should rarely give on-road problems if properly maintained. In order to enjoy trouble-free motoring in an older Mini it is wise to monitor the condition of mechanical and electrical components whenever you drive or service the car, and to try to predict which of them might give trouble before they do fail.

Some breakdowns are of course caused by unpredictable mechanical faults, such as seized gearboxes or engines, broken connecting rods and the like (please don't have nightmares about this happening to you – few people ever experience such major failures) although the vast majority of roadside breakdowns are caused by more avoidable failures of components in the fuel and particularly the ignition system rather than by terminal faults occurring in the engine or drive train. Merely supplementing your regular maintenance routine with a visual inspection of fuel lines (check for corrosion of the metal fuel pipes on older cars) and ignition wiring for cuts and abrasions can help to prevent many breakdowns.

The simple maintenance routines described in the earlier chapter will also go a long way to ward minimising the chances of a mechanical breakdown, but there are extra precautions which will not only help prevent breakdowns but also allow you to deal with them if they do arise.

It is well worth carrying a basic 'get you home' repair kit in the car at all times. The minimum such kit might consist of an adjustable spanner and preferably a set of imperial spanners, a spark plug box spanner, emery cloth, sturdy pliers with a built-in wire cutter, and a small selection of screwdrivers. Many suitable motorists' tool kits are available, and they are usually packaged in plastic carrying cases which not only keep the tools together, dry and in one place, but also stop them from rattling as the car is driven! Supplement this with a tow rope, jump leads, electrical insulation tape, a small selection of wire end terminals, self-tapping screws, fuses, lengths of wire, plus water for the radiator and perhaps a litre of engine oil. And, of course, a foot pump. In many countries you have by law to carry a warning triangle in the car at all times and, legal requirement or not, it is recommended that you keep one in the car boot.

Before you set out on a journey of any appreciable duration it is well worth taking a few seconds to carry out simple checks. Visually check the tyres for inflation, bulges and for any signs of damage. Check that the lights and brake lights work, and that the headlights are as bright as usual (the battery could be running down). When you turn the ignition key, note whether the engine turns over as quickly as usual and, when it fires up, check the oil low pressure warning light (where fitted) immediately to ensure that it goes off and keep an eye on the ignition light to ensure that it goes out, signifying that the battery is indeed being charged. Any new phenomena, such as blue smoke or steam – smoke slowly drifts away, steam disappears – from the exhaust (worn or broken piston rings, worn valve stems/guides allowing oil into cylinders or damaged head gasket/cracked head or block allowing in coolant – all require specialist attention) or unusual sounds when the engine fires up, are warning signs that all is not well, and remedial

ALWAYS carry out the easiest checks first. This car had a slipping clutch, and the clutch was removed for inspection. However, the cause turned out to be nothing more serious than a blocked engine breather pipe, which caused crankcase pressure to build up, forcing oil into the clutch housing. The breather pipe runs to the carb, which puts a constant vacuum into the crankcase, preventing pressure build-up. Had the dipstick not been such a close fit, incidentally, the oil would have probably come out of its hole rather than the clutch.

action should follow as soon as possible. A deep rumbling noise on first starting the engine could possibly be a not too serious fault such as a bracket retaining bolt having worked loose, allowing the component it holds to rattle about, or it could – and most probably does – indicate worn main/big end bearings. Seek professional assistance!

Preparing for a long journey is a more serious matter. The tyres (including the spare) should be checked with a gauge for correct inflation and they should be checked thoroughly for tread depth, cuts, abrasions and bulges. Check the tightness of the wheel nuts.

Lift the bonnet. Check the levels of the fluid in the brake and clutch reservoirs. If either is substantially low then it will pay to have the cause established and dealt with before a long journey is undertaken. If a level is down just a little then top it up. Check the engine oil level and again, if it is unduly low then seek and remedy the cause before undertaking a long journey, but top up if it has dropped just a little since last checked. Check the level in the windscreen washer bottle. Check the coolant level and top up if a little low but investigate if very much coolant is being lost. Examine the fan belt for cuts and general wear (a snapped fan belt is a very common cause of breakdowns – smart people carry a spare) and replace if necessary.

Start the engine, check the oil pressure warning light and ignition warning light, then check all electrical equipment for correct functioning, including the lighting system. It is not a bad idea also to check the battery electrolyte level.

Before setting out on a long journey it is

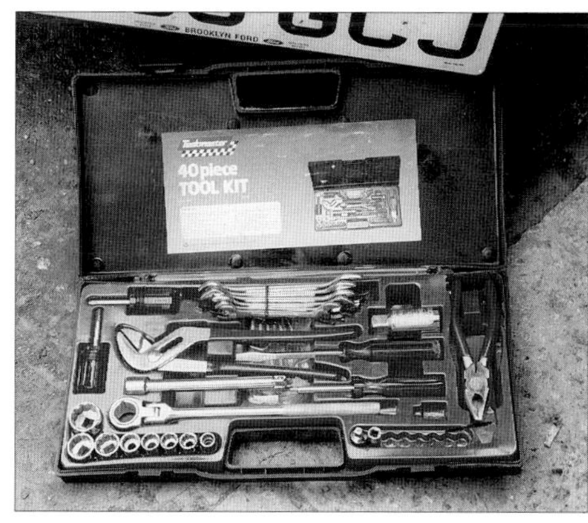

Small toolkits like this can prove worth their weight in gold if they allow you to fix a problem at the roadside rather than pay through the nose to be towed to the nearest garage!

worth obtaining a few spare parts which can often get you out of trouble. These are a fan belt, a distributor cap and points/condenser, spark plugs and their leads, and light bulbs. It is also a good idea to carry water for the radiator, a litre of oil, a spray can of light oil (for spraying onto the ignition components if they get wet, which they often do on Minis) and a small container of brake/clutch fluid.

Those who carry out no work on their cars themselves would do well to have their cars serviced and checked at a service centre immediately before embarking on a long journey. Membership of one of the national breakdown organizations would obviously also be a good precaution!

Those who do carry out even limited home servicing of their Minis can help avert breakdowns by checking components which might not normally be dealt with during a service. Examining the state of wiring can reveal signs of overheating which, if left unattended, could be the cause of an electrical fire. Examining the state of the fuel tank plus the fuel lines could reveal a small leak destined to turn into a substantial one if left to its own devices. Mini fuel tanks rarely leak because they are situated in the boot, safe from attack by the elements: if a leak is discovered, however, don't use the car until the problem has been dealt with. Even disconnecting the battery could result in a small electrical spark sufficient to cause an explosion if the boot is full of petrol vapours. Don't take any chances – open the boot lid to allow petrol vapours to escape, and bring in professional assistance.

An awareness of the sounds and smells of your car when underway is a priceless aid to predicting looming faults. Any new noise or unfamiliar aroma could turn out to be a symptom of an expensive (if not immediately remedied) fault or the cause of a future breakdown. Any apparent fault should be investigated at the earliest opportunity, and always remember that no mechanical nor electrical fault can ever 'cure' itself – if a suspicious noise suddenly stops, the chances are that far from the fault curing itself, it has entered the next stage of its progress towards complete breakdown.

FLAT TYRE

Most drivers will suffer a punctured tyre at some point in their motoring careers, and those who have never changed a wheel might care to take the precaution of practising doing so in the comfort and safety of their own driveway in preparation for the time they have to do it for real.

For a roadside wheel change, I make a point of putting the wheel under the sill – just in case the car slips from the jack.

Firstly, although you should never in normal circumstances drive a car which has a flat tyre, do get the car to a place of safety (driving as slowly as possible) before stopping. On the motorway this is the hard shoulder. On ordinary roads, don't drive miles looking for a lay-by, because the tyre will come off the rim and you'll destroy both tyre and wheel; find a straight section of road where other motorists can see you in plenty of time – never stop on a bend in the road. If you have a warning triangle or anything else which will warn drivers to slow down before they reach you, put it out. If your car is fitted with hazard warning lights, switch them on. At night, at the very least leave your side-lights on.

Get the spare wheel out and check that it's inflated properly. Engage the handbrake and place the car in gear. If you can find a couple of stones (or keep chocks in the car) for the front wheel which is to remain on the ground then use them. Slacken the wheel nuts, then jack up the offending side of the car, using the reinforced jacking point provided mid-way along the sill underside.

Remove wheel nuts, pull the wheel off, offer up the spare and re-fit the wheel nuts. Tighten these until the wheel is securely held, then lower the car to the ground and remove the jack. The wheel nuts now have to be finally tightened, and many people don't seem to know how much to tighten either! With wheel nuts, don't overdo it by jumping up and down on the end of the wheelbrace – remember that you will have to get them off again – firm pressure with your arm muscles will be perfectly sufficient. It is as well to check the tightness of wheel fixings after having driven the car for a few miles.

AN INTRODUCTION TO FUEL AND ELECTRICS

It is far easier to trace faults in the electrical and fuel delivery systems (the two major causes of roadside breakdowns) if you have a basic

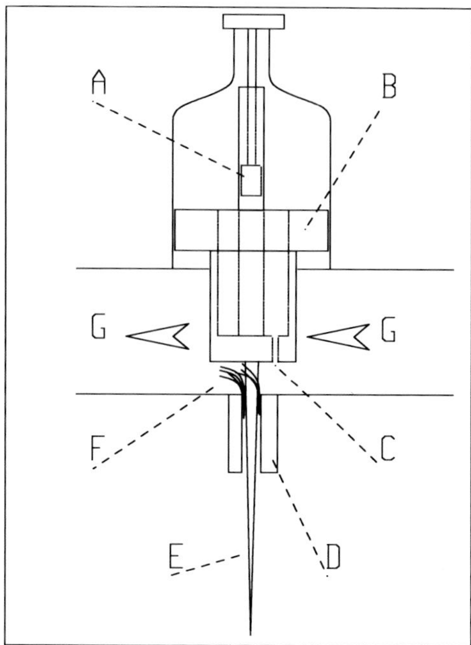

The workings of the SU HS2/4 carburettor. As air is drawn through the throat (G), its pressure decreases. A vacuum extends into the piston chamber (bell housing) above the piston (B) via the air filter adapter gasket (not shown), causing the piston to rise. The small hole (C) allows air under the piston, so that the greater force of the vacuum above the piston can lift it. The piston pulls the tapered needle (E) upwards, so increasing the effective surface area of the fuel in the main jet (D), so that more enters the airstream as fine droplets (F).

The HIF carburettors fitted to later cars are more complicated than the HS of early cars, though the basic principles of operation are the same. The main jet of the HIF carb is held by a bi-metallic bracket, which varies its height and hence the richness of the mixture, according to temperature. To vary the mixture, a screw on the main body acts on the bi-metallic bracket. Choke is provided by a separate jet.

A good workshop manual should include details of stripping and servicing the HIF.

understanding of how these work. Of the two, the fuel delivery system is the simpler, so we'll take a look at this first. The following is not a treatise on the workings of the automobile, but considers only specific areas which typically contribute to breakdowns.

CARBURETTORS

Petrol is stored in and drawn from the fuel tank by an electric (mounted on the subframe) or mechanical (integral with the engine) pump, which pushes it into a fuel bowl in the carburettor. A float within the fuel bowl operates a valve when the bowl becomes full, so cutting off the supply of fuel and preventing the engine from receiving too much fuel, i.e., flooding the cylinders. If the cylinders were to flood, the spark plug ends would become soaked and could not spark to ignite the mixture. The electric fuel pump automatically stops pumping when this happens.

As the engine turns over, air is drawn into it through the carburettor throat, in which the main jet is situated. There is petrol in the jet, and the effective diameter of the jet is controlled by a tapered needle which can rise and fall in accordance with the amount of air being drawn into the engine. As air rushes through the carburettor throat, its density and hence its pressure drops, and this causes two things to happen. Firstly, a piston (which holds the main jet needle) in the top of the carburettor (the dashpot) rises within the dashpot. This happens because an air passage connects the volume above the piston to the carburettor throat, and the reduction in air pressure in the throat draws air from the dashpot chamber, lowering its pressure and hence drawing the piston upwards. The piston draws the needle upwards with it, which effectively enlarges the opening in the main jet.

The second thing which happens is that the low pressure air rushing through the carburettor throat draws tiny droplets of petrol from the jet, so that a mixture of fine droplets of petrol and air enter the combustion chambers. This mixture is ignited by a sparking plug to provide the energy to power the car.

The choke operates by pulling the main jet downwards (HS2 carburettors) so that more fuel is drawn into the mixture in relation to the quantity of air, giving a 'rich' mixture to help start the engine on cold mornings.

The fuel system also contains fuel filters, which trap any foreign bodies in the fuel, such as tiny rust flakes from the inside of the fuel tank and any objects which might fall into the fuel tank filler neck when the car is being refuelled. We'll come back to the electric fuel pump after looking at the electricity which powers it.

FUEL INJECTION

From the mid-1960s onwards, concern about atmospheric pollution caused by motor cars resulted in efforts by motor manufacturers to reduce that pollution. Fuel tank breathers were fitted with carbon filters to scrub out hydrocarbons from evaporating petrol, fuel delivery systems had retrieval systems, air was pumped into exhaust manifolds to burn off un-burnt and partially burnt fuel, and crankcase breathers funnelled hydrocarbon fumes into the inlet manifold, so that they would burn in the engine.

The levels of hydrocarbons in the atmosphere most especially in and around some large North American cities reacted with strong sunlight and caused a photochemical smog, which lead to the introduction of legislation to reduce the levels of hydrocarbons emitted from cars. Also high on the pollution agenda were other polluting substances which are a by-product of the internal combustion engine – Carbon Monoxide (CO – a deadly gas) and Oxides Of Nitrogen (NOX). These can be dealt with by burning them in the exhaust manifold, but the technique does tend to rob the engine of power. In Europe, most efforts to reduce pollution were aimed at improving the efficiency of the combustion process, very often retaining carburettor fuel delivery. In North America, where pollution problems in specific areas were far more serious, some manufacturers opted for fuel injection systems. The Mini Cooper from 1991 has been fitted with fuel injection.

Fuel injection systems allow the amounts of fuel being delivered to vary more precisely according to demands than can carburation systems. There are two benefits to this; greater power can generally be achieved and exhaust emissions can be more precisely controlled. The down-side of fuel injection is its greater complexity in comparison with simple, user-repairable carburettors.

Fuel is pumped from the tank as in carburation systems but the injection system incorporates an accumulator (or regulator) which maintains the constant high pressure needed (which typically ranges from 25 psi to 100 psi depending on the type of injection system), because fuel atomisation is dependent upon it being pumped under high pressure through a jet (single point) or jets (multi-point). The accumulator also smoothes out individual fuel pump pulses to maintain a constant pressure, and it maintains some fuel pressure when the engine is switched off, so that adequate pressure is forthcoming immediately the engine is re-started.

There are essentially two types of fuel injection system. The earlier systems by and large employed simple mechanical operating methods common to contemporary diesel injection systems. An air flow sensing plate and lever operate the mechanical mixture control unit which enriches or weakens the mixture according to the amount of air being drawn into the engine. The mixture control unit contains a valve mechanism which is driven from the engine and which allows fuel into each injector as and when needed.

Electronic fuel injection systems incorporate an Electronic Control Unit (ECU). This is in effect a simple digital computer which reacts to electronic input signals from the distributor (to control injector opening timing), the accelerator pedal, the air temperature sensor and air pressure sensor, and which controls the various injectors' opening times and durations (electric, by solenoids), plus an extra air valve, which effectively bypasses the throttle butterfly, allowing a very lean mixture into the engine on the overrun.

ELECTRICS

The electrical system is more complicated to explain, and – with apologies to the many who will find the following beneath them or even so simplified as to verge on the misleading – we'll start at the very beginning by looking at what electricity is. You can't touch it, you can't smell or see it – so just what is electricity? Think of a length of copper wire at the atomic level. Each atom nucleus is surrounded by many orbiting electrons, some of which are not held in orbit too strongly by their nucleus. When no electrical current is flowing, some of these electrons become detached from their atoms and fly off to collide with other atoms which, in turn, can have one of their electrons knocked out of orbit. This movement of electrons is random. But when the two ends of the wire are connected to a battery, there exists a glut of electrons at one end and too few at the other, a potential difference which causes electrons to flow through the wire from one terminal to the other – in other words, the random flights of electrons have been replaced with a steady and directional flow.

When a copper wire which is part of a circuit passes through a magnetic field, a current is generated – the longer the wire, the greater the electrical force. This is how electricity is generated by the dynamo or alternator – lots of wire wound into a coil passing through a strong magnetic field.

So electricity can be defined as a controlled flow of electrons, but how is this put to use?

For cars, there are two side-effects of electrical current flow of interest; electricity flowing through a material generates heat and magnetic fields. Heat is generated when the flow reaches an area of resistance – a material whose atoms hold on to their electrons rather more tightly than do conductive materials such as copper, gold and silver. The resistive metals used in light bulbs are the most obvious example; run electricity through them and they get hot – so hot, in fact, that they give out bright light. Were they not surrounded in an inert gas inside the glass bulb which prevents combustion from occurring, then they would burn through in a fraction of a second. Other areas of resistance are corroded connections, a length of damaged wire with reduced cross section area, or a wire of too-small a cross sectional area – if it allows electricity to pass through but restricts the flow then it will become hot.

While on the subject of wires, the cross sectional area of wire must increase in accordance with the quantity of electricity it will have to handle. A side-light wire carries only a small current and so is of thin section wire while the starter motor wires carry a huge current and so they are very thick. If too much electricity is drawn through too thin a wire, the wire will quickly become hot, and burn off its insulation.

Magnetism is another matter. When current flows through a wire, a weak magnetic field is created around the wire. This is too low in power to be of any automotive use, but if the length of wire is coiled up so that a great length of wire occupies a small space, then the strength of the field is increased and can do a lot of work.

For our purposes, we'll consider two utilisations of electro-magnets. The starter solenoid is an electro-magnet which, when power flows through its coil, generates sufficient magnetic force to pull a metal bar which completes another electric circuit, but one which requires very high levels of energy – the starter motor circuit. The first section of the ignition system (from the ignition switch to the starter solenoid coil) carries only small currents, which is important not only because it saves having to run yards of heavy-duty cable but also for safety reasons. You turn on the ignition and the ignition circuit is energised, turn the key a little more and the starter solenoid completes a heavy-duty circuit to turn the starter motor.

The second electro-magnet operated component to consider is the electric fuel pump. Two simple flaps (non-return valves) allow petrol into and out of a chamber, depending on whether there is suction or pressure. The suction which draws petrol from the tank and the pressure which pushes it towards the carburettors is provided by a diaphragm which moves backwards and forwards to vary the volume of the chamber. The diaphragm is powered by an electromagnet driving a moveable metal core.

When the carburettor float drops and opens the valve to accept fuel from the pump, the metal core and with it the diaphragm is pushed forwards by a spring, pushing fuel out of the chamber and towards the carburettor. When the diaphragm and metal core are fully forwards, this closes a set of points (electrical contacts) at the rear of the unit, completing a circuit which energises the electro-magnet. This pulls the core, and hence the diaphragm, backwards, sucking petrol into the chamber. When the core is fully back, the points open, the electro-magnet is 'off' and the spring pushes the core and diaphragm forwards, pushing petrol from the outlet, until the points again close and the process is re-started. When the fuel bowl is full and the inlet is sealed, the pressure in the pump outlet pipe is great enough to stop the spring from pushing forwards. Next time you switch on the ignition first thing in the morning, listen for the clicking noise made by the fuel pump.

Some Minis are fitted with a mechanical fuel pump. This is situated on the side of the engine block, and is driven via a lever by the camshaft.

Onto the battery. Most people believe that

the car battery stores electricity – wrong! The car battery houses metallic and chemical substances which, when a load (a light bulb or starter motor etc.) is connected, begin a reversible chemical process. Inside the battery are a number of cells each containing two dissimilar metal plates in a weak acid solution (electrolyte). When you throw a switch and complete the circuit between the two terminals, electrons flow from one type of plate to the other, changing the chemical composition of each and in the process generating a small electrical current of just over two volts. A six volt battery contains three cells, a twelve volt battery contains six.

The chemical process in a car battery is reversible; that is, when the generator (dynamo or alternator) creates an electrical current, some is fed to the battery and reverses the process so that the two metals return to their former composition, 're-charging' the battery.

To save on wiring, the chassis (body) of the car, being composed of metal which conducts electricity, is substituted for one of the wires needed to complete a circuit. The body in this respect is known as the 'earth' (UK) or 'ground' (USA). So, a wire runs from a terminal, through a switch to a device – a light bulb or whatever – through the device, into the bodyshell and back to the other terminal, which is connected to the body by the earth strap. Regarding earths, the electric currents in a circuit actively seek these out because they are the channel of least resistance back to the

A simplified diagram of the ignition circuit. The points are shown open, when the capacitor (above the points and cam within the distributor) comes into play.

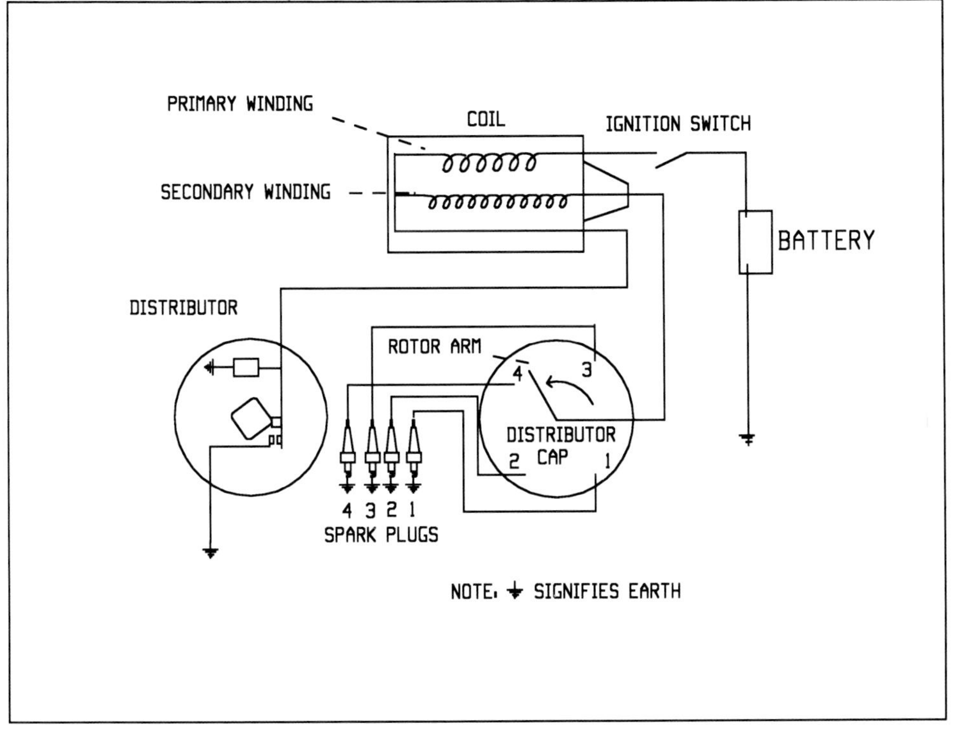

The insides of the ignition coil. The two windings are concentric – in wiring diagrams they are usually shown side by side.

battery – if a wire leading to a light bulb, for instance, shorts to earth, then the current will take this easier route rather than pass through the light bulb, in the process, drawing excessive current and blowing a fuse or damaging the wiring.

We've looked at electricity, wires and batteries; what next? The ignition system (which causes more breakdowns than anything else).

When you operate the ignition key, the ignition circuit energises a coil of wire called the primary winding within the body of the ignition coil. Also within the coil is a second winding called – wait for it – the secondary winding, which has many times more individual coils than the primary winding. A strong magnetic field builds up around the primary winding and, when the circuit which feeds it is broken, the magnetic field collapses and induces an electrical charge in the secondary winding. The secondary winding contains far more wire than the primary, and is in fact around a mile in length, which has the effect of 'stepping up' the voltage. The voltage created when the magnetic field collapses is many times higher – 25,000 volts – which is sufficiently high to be able to jump across small gaps to find an earth. Both windings are cooled by oil contained within the coil casing. The coil can overheat – incidentally – and its case split if the ignition is left switched on for long periods with the points closed and the engine not running. So far so good.

Inside the distributor, the points are closed and it is these which complete the circuit to earth which energises the primary winding in the coil. As the engine turns over, one of the distributor drive shaft cam lobes opens the points, so breaking that circuit, so that the magnetic field of the primary winding breaks down, generating the high voltage in the secondary winding, which immediately looks for an earth, escaping into the main coil to the distributor High Tension lead. The primary circuit may have been broken by the points opening, but the residual electric charge in the primary coil is quite strong enough to jump across the points to find an earth. As you will remember, areas of resistance generate heat, and the air gap in the points is one such area.

Because having electricity jump across the points between two thousand and ten thousand times a minute (at engine revolutions of 1,000 rpm and 5,000 rpm respectively) would rapidly burn away the points, the distributor is fitted with a condenser. This contains two rolled-up sheets of conductive metal, separated by an insulator, so that the two cannot touch. The residual electric charge in the primary coil doesn't know this, and rushes into the condenser thinking that it is an earth instead of jumping the gap between the points, so saving the points. Once the charge gets into the condenser, it realises it's been duped (determined but blinkered, these electrical charges) and, because the points will by then have closed again to complete the circuit, it turns around and heads back for the primary winding and helps energise it ready for the next time that the points open.

At the very same time, the rotor arm in the distributor is whizzing round and round, past the terminals in the distributor cap to which the sparking plug high tension leads are connected. It is adjacent to each terminal as the points are opening and the 25,000 volts are headed up the main high tension lead for the charge to sense a path to earth. The high tension lead from the coil tower (along which the charge from the winding is running) leads via the centre of the distributor cap and a carbon contact to the metal strip on the top of the rotor arm, and the charge jumps across into the sparking plug high tension lead terminal and heads off in the direction of the spark plug, trying to find an earth to complete the circuit. When it gets there, it finds that it has to jump yet another gap (the spark plug gap) to get to earth, in so doing, providing the spark to ignite the fuel/air mixture within the cylinder. Pretty straightforward?

ENGINE WON'T START

The least traumatic place to suffer a breakdown is on the drive at home, and happily, this is where the majority of breakdowns reportedly occur. Carry out the simplest checks first and leave the fancy stuff till later.

ENGINE REFUSES TO TURN OVER

If the ignition light dims as the key is turned but no noise emanates from the starter motor, then check the battery connections. Another sure sign of poor battery connections is when you turn the key, there is a muted clunk from the engine bay, and the ignition light fails to come back on. A loose or corroded connection can in some instances supply enough power for, say, the lights, but not enough for the starter motor. Also check the earth strap/bodywork connection for tightness and corrosion.

If the connections are good, the chances are that the battery is run down, meaning either that it is in poor condition and unable to hold a charge, that you left the lights switched on overnight or that the generator is not delivering a full charge. You can check whether the battery is nearly flat by switching on the headlights and adjudging their brightness. Check the electrolyte level; if it is substantially down then the generator is probably over-charging the battery – in the case of a dynamo, the regulator needs attention, alternators should be exchanged.

While you can bump start the car or use jumper leads to get a car with a flat battery going, you should not travel anywhere other than to a place of repair unless you possess a multi meter and are able to check that the battery is being charged.

If the battery seems OK, check the connections to the starter solenoid and the starter motor. Remove the spade connector from the solenoid and clean this – tiny traces of corrosion can act as very effective insulation. Have an assistant operate the ignition switch while you listen for the starter solenoid 'click'. The solenoid, as we have already established, is an electrically operated switch which carries the huge current needed by the starter motor and which is activated by a very small current from the ignition switch. If, after you cleaned the connection, it still isn't operating, try giving it a sharp tap with a spanner or similar (car out of gear – keep clear of moving parts), and try again.

If the solenoid is operating (you can hear it click), then the starter motor may be jammed – more common with inertia starters. If so, place the car in fourth gear (ignition OFF), disengage the handbrake and rock the car forwards and backwards, which can often free a jammed starter. Alternatively, give the body of the motor a clout with a mallet. If the engine still won't turn over, you'll have to replace the solenoid or replace/repair the starter motor as appropriate – either way, you ain't going anywhere. The problem could be cured with new starter motor brushes or pinion, or in the worst scenario it could necessitate replacement of the flywheel ring gear, so seek professional advice.

ENGINE TURNS OVER BUT WON'T FIRE

Don't just sit there churning the engine over – all you'll accomplish by this is running the battery flat.

Is there fuel in the tank? Is there an aroma of petrol from the exhaust tail pipe just after the engine has been turned over? – if so, fuel is reaching the engine and the fault probably lies with the ignition. Turn the ignition switch off and raise the bonnet. You're going to have to get your hands dirty.

IGNITION

Check the connections at either end of the main HT lead running from the coil to the distributor cap. Check the other wires attached to the coil, and remake any poor connections. Check the high tension leads and distributor cap – if these have moisture on them then dry them off because they are allowing the charge which should go to the spark plugs to go to earth instead – and spray or preferably use a cloth to wipe on a thin coating of light oil and then try again to start the car. If the engine still refuses to fire, switch off the ignition, pull the main HT feed from the distributor cap and hold this gently (if you possess the proper insulated pliers for the job – otherwise, try to tape it into position) a fraction of an inch from a good earth, well away from the fuel supply and the spark plug holes.

Get an assistant to turn the engine over for a couple of seconds and observe whether a spark can be seen to jump between the HT lead and the earth – accompanied by an audible clicking sound. If not, then either the coil or its feed is probably the cause. If there is a spark, then (ignition switch off) replace the HT lead in the distributor cap, remove the distributor cap and inspect it minutely for cracks which could contain moisture. Also check for signs of arcing – rough-edged black lines which contain carbon which forms a highly conductive path for electricity and channels it away from the correct spark plug. A temporary repair can be effected by scratching out the carbon, but the distributor cap should be replaced. Check that the points open and close freely

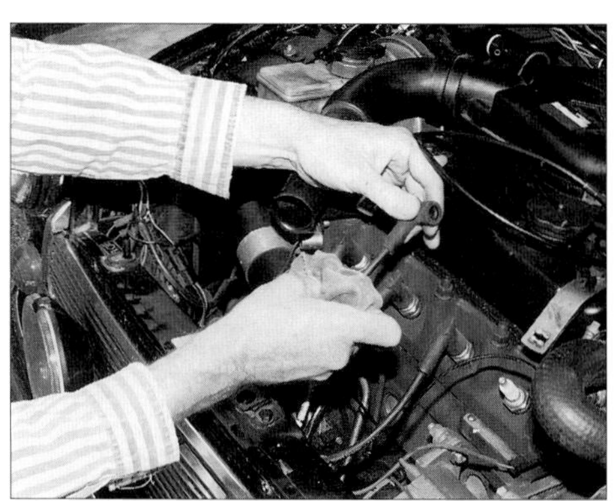

Damp on the distributor, plug leads/spark plugs. This can direct the HT voltage to earth rather than through the spark plugs. If the car won't start on a wet morning, or dies after driving through a ford or rainstorm, dry off the cap and leads.

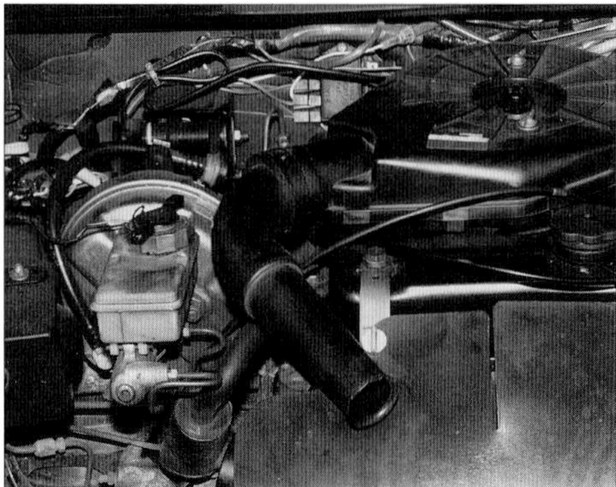

More recent Minis are fitted with this splash guard, which keeps water off the ignition components. I once drove a Mini 1000 through the worst thunderstorm and consequent flash flooding I've ever known – the Mini kept going even after I saw a Land Rover judder to a halt with wet ignition components.

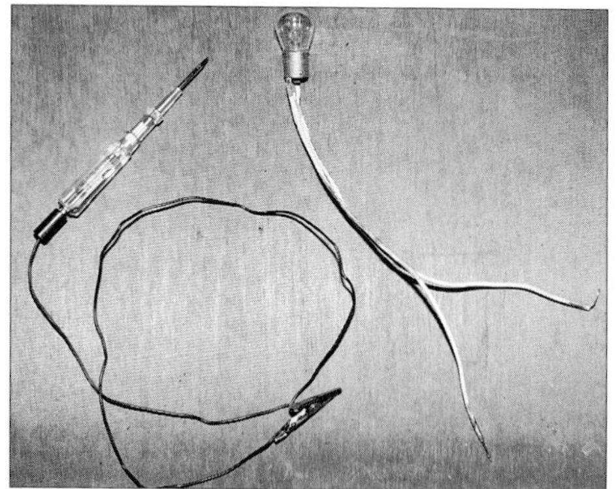

You can buy small bulb-type electrical testers to see whether power is available at points throughout a circuit. I made up this one simply by soldering wires to a light bulb.

Checking for power at coil. If there's no spark, a simple bulb-type tester like this will allow you to establish whether the coil is receiving power.

and that their contacts are clean and not heavily pitted. If the points are dirty, clean them and try to start the engine.

When starting a car using the choke, more than at any other time, the rich fuel/air mixture in the cylinders needs a good, strong spark from the plugs. Loose plug end fittings cause a loss of electrical energy to the sparking plugs and hence a weak spark, so check that the end fittings are all tight. If these are found to be loose, remove the spark plugs and dry off their ends – they will be covered with petrol.

Remove and check the spark plugs visually for obvious damage such as cracked ceramics,

Don't hold a sparking plug when testing it – you'll get a belt if you do! Either use insulated pliers, or tape it to an earth well away from the spark plug holes.

The starter solenoid. If you don't hear a click from this when you turn the ignition key, giving the body of the solenoid a clout with a screwdriver handle or something similar can free it.

for heavy carbon deposits (wire brush this off, and make a note to have the carburation set – the engine is running too rich), sticky black deposits (clean off but make a note to investigate at the first opportunity why oil is finding its way into the cylinders – could be broken or worn piston rings, valve stem to valve guide clearance), glazing (engine running far too hot – get professional advice and don't run the engine in this state), and correct gap (adjust). Then place each plug in turn in its lead and tape it to a good earth away from the fuel delivery system, carburettors and plug holes (or hold it using the proper insulated pliers) and have the engine turned over to see whether there is a spark. Absence of a spark could be due to a faulty plug or lead, so try apparently faulty plugs on other leads to establish which is at fault: replace any faulty plugs or leads.

FUEL

NOTE: Where the following information relates to fuel delivery problems, it pertains primarily to carburettor-equipped Minis: problems with fuel injection systems really demand professional attention. Before booking your injected Cooper in for a diagnostic test, though, do take the time to go over the ignition system just to make sure that the 'fuel' problem isn't caused by ignition faults – many are. Also, check valve clearances, and check for engine air induction; because the inlet manifold air flow determines the amount of fuel which is injected, air induction fools the system into thinking that less fuel is needed than is actually the case.

Fuel delivery problems are far less common causes of non-starting engines than ignition faults. If your Mini has an electric pump, pull the main fuel line from the carburettor (it is as well to wrap a cloth around the pipe end before removing it because if the pump is working then there will be residual pressure in the system) and place the end in a jar or similar container while an assistant turns the ignition switch on (so that the ignition light comes on – there is no need to spin the engine) for a second or two. If fuel pumps from the line, then replace it on the carburettor. If no fuel is forthcoming, check the in-line fuel filter (where fitted, generally to later cars – although a blocked filter should have been apparent as a developing fault – lumpy running, intermittent loss of power – for some time) and suspect a faulty pump. A sharp tap on the pump body can sometimes rectify sticking points, although it is recommended that the pump is attended to at the earliest opportunity before it lets you down again.

To check a mechanical pump, the line is again pulled from the carburettor and held in a container, but this time, the engine has to be turned over for a few seconds in order that the pump operates. If no fuel is forthcoming, you're in trouble because the fuel pump is one of the many inaccessible components on the Mini – in this case, tucked away under the exhaust manifold. Bad luck! Incidentally, if the engine oil on the dipstick smells strongly of petrol then the fuel pump diaphragm is at fault – some are repairable, some are sealed units. Consult a workshop manual.

If fuel is available but the engine still won't start, then it could be flooded, which should have been apparent when you inspected the (wet, smelling strongly of petrol) spark plugs. The engine can flood because either the choke jams or too much choke has been applied for the conditions, because the carburettor float jams or most commonly the inlet needle is held open by dirt. It is easy to check that the choke operates correctly – watch the jet holder come down as someone operates the control. To clear dirt from the inlet valve, pinch the fuel line with the engine turning over so that the float chamber fuel level drops – then release the line and the gush of fuel through the inlet valve will normally do the trick. If this fails, the float could be mal-adjusted (not all are adjustable) or leaking (it sinks).

Fuel injection Cooper

DO NOT try to test for fuel delivery, because the fuel pressure is maintained from 25 psi upwards, even when the engine is switched off and, if you were to start tinkering with the fuel lines, the fuel could spray everywhere. DON'T TOUCH IT!

STARTER MOTOR WORKS BUT DOES NOT TURN ENGINE

With inertia starters, check the condition of the battery – a flat battery cannot spin the motor quickly enough to engage the drive mechanism. Check that the starter motor mounting bolts are holding it securely and, if so, the problem is probably a sticking pinion or a broken drive spring. You could bump start the car, but what if you managed to stall it at the traffic lights? Best to forget using the car until the problem has been rectified.

ENGINE STARTS, BUT RUNS LUMPILY AND BACKFIRES WHEN REVVED

This is not a common fault, but can occur when one or more spark plugs or leads are duff. Un-burnt fuel mixture from the affected cylinder(s) passes into the exhaust manifold, where it can be ignited by hot or still-burning gasses from other cylinders which causes it to explode, and hence the backfiring. Check each plug and lead in turn as already described for a spark.

ENGINE WANTS TO FIRE BUT WON'T RUN

This is normally a sign of fuel starvation, caused by a blocked fuel filter, non-functioning choke on cold mornings or air induction. Check the fuel delivery as already described,

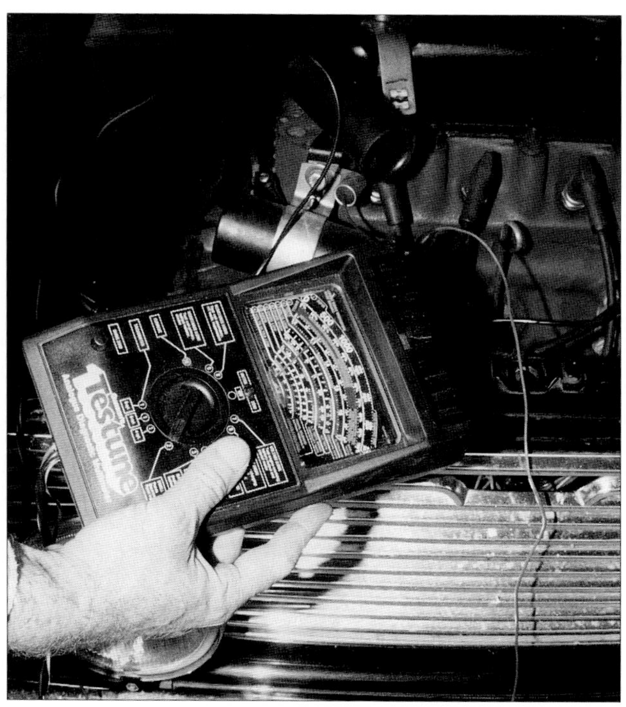

The little Gunson's tester I use can show dwell angle – the amount of time the points are closed. A fluctuating dwell angle causes similar fluctuations in ignition timing and is caused by a worn-out distributor.

The Crypton or a similar system not only allows mixture to be set spot-on, but can trace almost any ignition fault.

check that the choke cable pulls the jet down and check the vacuum advance pipe connection on the inlet manifold.

ENGINE TICKS OVER POORLY ON THREE CYLINDERS BUT ALL FOUR FIRE WHEN REVVED

This is normally caused by a break in a copper cored plug lead. A breakage can occur which is temporarily 'welded' as the engine revs but breaks again on tickover when engine movement is more exaggerated. Disconnect each lead in turn until the faulty one is found.

UNRELIABLE STARTERS/'PROBLEM' CARS

I seems that some cars are never to be relied upon to start first time every time. Some won't start with the engine cold; others with the engine hot. Some cars never seem to give their best and can appear un-tuneable. In either case, give the car a major service, which entails replacing most ignition components and setting up the timing and carburation correctly (the carburation is best set by professionals; remember that all UK MOT testing stations now have exhaust gas analysers with which they can get it spot on).

Also, replace any filters in the fuel delivery system and check the (electric) fuel pump points for corrosion which could cause intermittent fuel delivery problems. If this fails to cure the problems, exchange the fuel pump.

If you don't feel able to do this then have the car serviced by a specialist. It is worth having the cylinder compression checked (this only takes a few minutes and won't cost too much) or buying a meter and testing it yourself. If one or more cylinders are substantially down, then squirt a little engine oil through the spark plug hole and re-test. The oil will temporarily improve the piston ring seal and, if the compression rises with the addition of the oil, the fault is connected with the piston rings and/or worn cylinder bores (a re-bore and oversize pistons are needed) – if there is no change then the valves are the culprit and a cylinder head overhaul is required.

Checking the ignition timing with a Crypton only takes a couple of minutes. Rather than have a specific fault checked, it is worth asking the mechanic to give the car a 'tune' – meaning mixture and ignition.

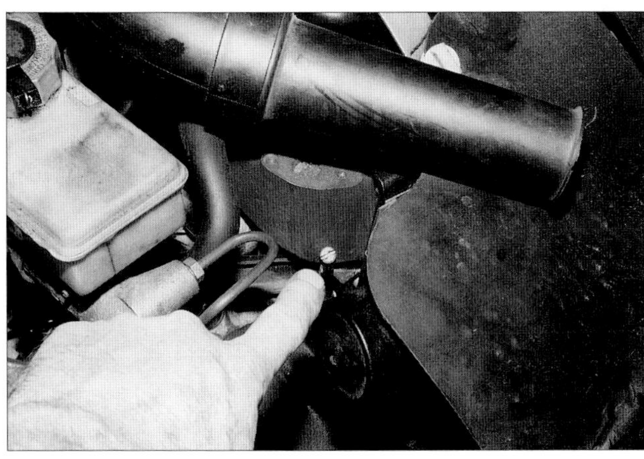

On recent Minis with catalytic converters, this plugged pipe runs from the exhaust down pipe for exhaust gas sampling.

Provided that an A series engine is reasonable condition – the cylinder head is not carbonned or cracked, the head gasket is intact and the valves and their seats not damaged (all of which will be revealed during a simple decoke) – fundamental problems with major fuel or ignition components are the most likely cause of unreliable starting, intermittent performance/high fuel consumption, pinking and other long-term problems.

Given that the engine (which, if suspect, can be swapped for an exchange reconditioned unit) is in good condition and that no apparent faults lie in the ignition or fuel delivery systems, many long-term problems can be cured by exchanging the distributor or the carburettor for reconditioned units. Typical faults include air induction through the carburettor throttle spindle bushes (which, on a reconditioned carburettor, will have been reamed out and re-bushed) and wear in the distributor. A rough and ready check for air induction via the throttle spindle is to spray a little carburettor cleaner, WD40 or even engine oil onto the spindle ends. This temporarily seals them (if they are leaking) and if the engine now runs at higher tickover revolutions then you have traced the cause of the problem.

Distributor wear can be traced by checking the dwell angle with a good automotive multi-meter (the dwell angle is the percentage or angle of the distributor shaft rotation during which the points are closed, when the coil primary winding is charging) – a fluctuating dwell angle reading indicates wear in the distributor shaft bearings and results in equal variations in ignition timing. Too small a dwell angle gives a weak spark.

Both air induction and distributor faults should become apparent if you book your car in for a session on a Crypton or similar. An experienced technician with such equipment should be able to pinpoint the cause of any such problems.

If you possess an automotive multi-meter then there is very little in the ignition system which you cannot test to find faults. Probably the most frequently used scale is the resistance reading (ohms) which allows you to locate disconnections (open circuits), test the coil windings and various connections. Working as a voltmeter, a multi-meter can be used to measure voltage drop across components and connections. Perhaps more importantly, it can measure voltage drop across the points when connected to the low tension lead and a good earth – anything more than 0.3V is unacceptable and usually indicates resistance across the points or occasionally between the base plate and the distributor body. Automotive multi-meters don't cost too much, and are well worth investing in. The author uses a Gunson Test Tune which, in addition to tracing simple open circuits (disconnections) can be used to test battery condition and charging, dwell angle, voltage drop and earth leakage. Costing less than a full professional service, such meters are highly recommended.

Air induction can be difficult to pin down because the air could – assuming all fastenings are tight – be entering via a damaged inlet manifold gasket or the carburettor via the throttle spindle, the vacuum advance pipe or – on recent Minis – the brake servo vacuum pipe. The usual symptom of air induction is lumpy tickover. Obviously, a portable exhaust gas tester will allow you to discover any such symptoms, although a throttle spindle leak can be proven by putting a little carburettor oil on the spindle ends as already described which – if there is induction – will make the mixture richer.

ON-ROAD BREAKDOWNS

The first rule of dealing with breakdowns on the road is not to panic, but to ensure that the car is parked in a safe place. In the case of a motorway this means the hard shoulder, and for safety's sake it is best to get any passengers out of the car and up the embankment. On ordinary roads as well as motorways, set out a warning triangle to advertise the presence of your car in plenty of time for following drivers, especially if you are unable to get the car fully off the road.

Once you are satisfied that everything is safe, investigate the fault. Unless the fault can be traced and rectified quickly, it is advisable to try to summon assistance at the earliest opportunity. You can waste hours fruitlessly looking for fuel or ignition faults (the most common causes of breakdowns), only to eventually discover that a component has totally failed and that repair is impossible without replacement.

A breakdown can become an emergency if, for instance, you continue to drive while the signs of a potential electrical fault are there, or if the car should come to a halt on a narrow road in thick fog. Again, don't panic, but try to move the car to a safer position, set out a warning triangle for other road users and get any passengers out of harm's way.

ENGINE 'DIES' OR LOSES POWER

The most common breakdown is when the engine dies or slowly loses power, and – terminal engine problems excepted – this will be due to a fault with either the ignition or the fuel delivery system. Before trying to trace the fault, examine the ignition wiring and the fuel system under the bonnet, the battery and fuel tank in the boot for danger signs, such as smoke from burning wire insulation or neat fuel which may have escaped from a fuel line or the carburettor. If there is a strong smell of petrol under the bonnet, in the boot, inside the car or underneath the car then clear passengers and bystanders from the vicinity and summon assistance. If all appears safe, then begin to trace the fault.

If you have just driven through a heavy rain storm, puddle or ford then check first for damp which allows the charge in the high tension leads to earth itself. If the high tension leads or their caps, the distributor or any other part of the ignition system is wet then simply dry it off with a clean cloth, spray on a little water repellent oil if you carry it in the car and try to start the engine.

In dry conditions, if the engine died suddenly without any warning signs then the fault (if electrical) obviously affects all four plugs at once – look firstly for a disconnection within the ignition circuit, starting at the distributor to coil HT lead and moving back through the system. If the engine misfired before losing power or stopping then start by checking the spark plug caps, then move backwards through the ignition circuit. Bear in mind that ignition faults are most probably the single greatest cause of breakdowns, and check this out first. If no ignition fault can be traced, then the problem may lie with the fuel delivery. The carburettor is in relatively close proximity to the hot exhaust manifold and down pipe, and you should always let these cool before doing anything to the carburettors or fuel lines. There is a strong argument at this stage for calling in assistance, if you have not already done so. Clear any passengers from the car, and quickly check for leakage in the fuel lines.

Fuel delivery problems usually mean that either no fuel is being delivered to the carburettors or that too much fuel is being taken in by the carburettors. The former fault usually lies with the fuel pump, or a blocked filter (or most commonly an empty fuel tank!) and the latter with a sticking float. Unless you know what you are doing, call for assistance.

ENGINE DIES A MILE INTO JOURNEY

If the engine has a habit of stopping a mile or so into your journey in cold, wet weather, the problem is usually icing. When air is drawn down through the carburettor throat, its pressure drops. One side-effect of this is that its temperature also drops – to freezing. Now, if the air being drawn into the carburettor is humid, the water droplets can freeze into ice, which usually builds up inside the inlet manifold. The build-up of ice restricts the effective internal diameter of the manifold, the engine does not receive enough fuel/air mixture and, unless the revs are kept up, the engine will die.

This phenomenon is known as 'icing' and you can usually prevent it by moving the carburettor air intake to the winter setting. If the engine stops altogether a mile or so into your journey, don't try to start the engine straight away. Leave it for a few minutes and heat within the engine compartment will melt the ice and the engine will re-start. Those who, a mile into their daily journey, are caught in traffic, might find that the engine regularly dies from icing – if so, pre-heat the engine compartment; run the engine for a couple of minutes, then leave it for a further couple of minutes, before starting the journey.

ENGINE LOSES POWER AND STOPS

Unless you have run out of fuel (in which case the engine would have been coughing and spluttering for a short time before it stopped) then you could have a disconnection or component failure in the ignition system (check as for engine which won't start) or, alternatively, fuel flow might be intermittent. The causes of this can be a blocked fuel tank breather (remove the filler cap and listen for a rush of air into the filler neck) a dirty fuel filter or fuel pump problems.

The engine could be overheating, in which case the coolant temperature gauge should have forewarned you of the problem. Let the engine cool before checking the coolant level.

ENGINE STOPS WITHOUT WARNING

This is almost invariably caused by an ignition fault. Check this as already described.

BREAKDOWN SERVICES

Some breakdown causes cannot be fixed at the roadside, and if you are unable to quickly establish the fault then it is advisable to summon assistance at the earliest opportunity. I reported a non-starting car (NOT a Mini) to one breakdown company at around 9.00 am one day when I was away from home and did not have access to the necessary tools to trace the fault myself. The breakdown service concerned relied on local garages to respond to any calls (I'm now a member of a club which uses its own recovery vehicles). The one-man-band they contacted in my case (a Sunday) was out playing golf, and eventually arrived at 6.00 pm – nine hours after the fault was reported!

My advice is to enrol in a service which is recommended by classic car magazines or the Mini Owners' Club because, if you are let down by such a company, then you can report the incident to the press or club and usually obtain some form of redress. Don't rely on back-street operations, but always choose a reputable, nation-wide operation; preferably one which has its own fleet of breakdown vehicles rather than relying on garages.

Always opt for a service which offers special memberships for classic car owners, because many operations won't cover, for instance, cars over ten years of age. Buy the best you can.

DEVELOPING PROBLEMS

Many problems develop slowly and even those faults which have serious consequences will often only be apparent from their symptoms i.e., side-effects. For instance, a partially blocked fuel filter can make the mixture too lean and, in time, this can wreck the engine unless rectified. The symptom which will be most apparent is engine overheating. The same symptom, however, can equally signal too-advanced ignition timing, a loose fan belt, coolant loss, blocked radiator and a host of other faults.

When a symptom such as overheating becomes apparent, its cause should be traced and rectified as soon as possible.

Not every developing fault encountered on a journey will necessarily lead to a breakdown before the destination is reached, although there are several problems which can arise which should be investigated the moment it is safe to stop the car. Such faults include a sudden drop in oil pressure, an unexplained rise in coolant temperature or any apparent electrical fault, whether constant or intermittent. All of these faults can lead in a very short space of time to serious (and invariably expensive) problems. A drop in oil pressure might allow the engine to run long enough to get you to your destination, but you could wreck the engine in the process. A rise in coolant temperature is not a fault in itself but a symptom of a serious fault which could cause extensive engine damage if left unattended. An electrical fault could start an electrical fire at any time, so take these very seriously indeed.

Any unusual noises warrant investigation at the earliest opportunity. In addition to engine noises such as knocking or pinking, listen for new noises from the transmission or suspension, and for suddenly excessive road/tyre noise (which may be accompanied by steering wheel vibration – which also warrants early investigation).

Pinking (a harmless-sounding tinkling noise which is usually heard with the engine under load) could be caused by air induction and hence a weak mixture, by too-advanced ignition, engine overheating (non-functioning thermostat or faulty water pump) or by several other faults – the noise is made by the pistons as they tip in the bore because the mixture is being ignited too early – the long-term consequences are very expensive, so get it seen to at the earliest opportunity.

Knocking is caused by the fuel/air mixture detonating – exploding, if you like – rather than burning in a controlled manner, and the knocking noise is actually made by the shock wave hitting the cylinder walls. Mixture detonation can be caused by a very weak mixture or if some dolt inadvertently puts standard unleaded in the tank. A knocking engine is not long for this world, so stop it as soon as is consistent with safety.

Sometimes, these warning signs lead to problems which can be dealt with there and then, sometimes, it is up to the driver to decide whether to carry on and risk damage to the car or whether to summon assistance. Of the faults which can be dealt with, if the engine is pinking, look firstly for an induction air leak. If an irregular knocking noise can be heard, check the tightness of exhaust, suspension and other fittings. If tyre noise can be heard or if vibration is suddenly felt through the steering wheel, check the tyres for bulges or other damage, and fit the spare to the appropriate corner.

TRANSMISSION/SUSPENSION NOISES

Idler Gear Howl

Drive passes from the crankshaft to the gearbox first motion (input) shaft via three gears, which can sometimes be heard at tickover, which is not necessarily a problem. If you can hear a howl when driving at speed, have the idler gears checked out professionally, or consult a workshop manual. But be warned, although you can accomplish this job with the engine in situ – it can be a swine!

Clutch Release Bearing Squeal

The clutch release bearing is packed with grease; when this has all gone, the bearing can squeal as the clutch operates. You can change the bearing (and it makes sense to replace the clutch at the same time) with the engine in situ but, having myself spent over a day in the past trying get the flywheel off a 1275GT, I would recommend that the engine is taken out, and that the opportunity is taken to attend to the idler gear bearings, clutch and clutch release bearing.

Clicking Outer Universal Joints (UJs)

If you hear a clicking from the front of the car at slow speed and near-full lock (such as manoeuvring in a car park) the culprit is the driveshaft outer UJs. Replacing these is not too difficult (though it pays to consult a workshop manual to make sure you will be comfortable with the job), so the labour charges if the job is farmed out to professionals should not be too great.

Thump on pulling away from a standstill

The inner UJs are usually the culprit here; a tad more difficult to replace than outer UJs; study your workshop manual and, if the job frightens you, it should not be too expensive to have it carried out professionally.

OVERHEATING

Why are roadworks always accompanied by signs which state that such and such an authority apologises for any delay caused when we all know perfectly well that roadworks are sited and timed to cause maximum delays to the greatest number of drivers? To make matters worse, and on a personal note, they always choose the hottest days of the year to resurface roads on which I want to drive – risking an overheated engine in the slow moving queue of traffic caused by said resurfacing. I strongly suspect a conspiracy.

It's not just roadworks which can cause on-road delays and consequent engine overheating. I – along, it seemed, with several other thousand Mini enthusiasts – approached Silverstone from the West when attending Mini 35. Big mistake. An hour to travel the last eight miles to the circuit and in blisteringly hot weather to boot. In this monumental queue, overheated Minis were dropping by the wayside – bonnets raised, steam issuing forth. Strangely, the Mini owners in the queue seemed almost to be lapping up this shared adversity – maybe the party spirit helped.

Like many cars, the Mini was launched in a period when traffic was much lighter, when roadworks seemed more infrequent and when the only queue of any real substance you'd find on a blisteringly hot bank holiday in England was on the then infamous Exeter bypass. Like many cars, Minis are intended to take advantage of a steady flow of air through the radiator and around the engine to help with the cooling and, if you leave them stationary with the engine running on a hot day for any period of time the temperature gauge will begin to creep in the wrong direction.

An overheated engine can blow its core plugs (all coolant lost and engine wrecked if not immediately turned off), it can boil its coolant and blow the radiator cap off or the radiator up (same resultse). Even nastier things can happen, but I'm sure you get the general idea that your engine must keep its cool.

Mild overheating can be counteracted by turning the heater and blower up full – hell on a hot day unless the car is fitted with a full length sunroof. More serious overheating demands that the engine is stopped. This can cause a temporary traffic jam, but the alternative is to let the engine coolant boil, the engine seize and cause a more permanent jam. Pull off the road anywhere safe, turn off the engine and raise the bonnet. DON'T move the radiator cap before the engine has fully cooled unless you enjoy getting third-degree scalds, and never pour cold water into a hot engine.

The worst place to have an overheating engine is in a queue on a motorway when the hard shoulder has been pressed into service as an extra lane. There is simply nowhere to go, and you have the choice of risking a real breakdown and causing a temporary one by switching off the ignition.

Some people remove the thermostat in an attempt to counteract anticipated overheating – mistake. True, the temperature gauge usually responds by showing a lower engine coolant temperature, but nasty things are happening inside the engine. Numbers three and (especially) four cylinders are being robbed of coolant and getting even hotter than before as a consequence!

If you anticipate being caught up in heavy traffic during the summer, you could consider fitting a lower temperature thermostat to help alleviate overheating. Always ensure that the coolant level is OK and that the fan belt is in excellent condition and correctly tensioned before setting out on a long journey.

Before fitting a cooler thermostat, check out the ignition timing, the carb and manifold for air induction and the mixture strength. Also flush out the radiator.

TROUBLE SHOOTING

The following notes omit one potential cause of every one of the problems listed – major mechanical failure. Remember – if a fault cannot be traced quickly, it is best to summon assistance rather than waste time looking for a problem which you might not be able to deal with at the roadside.

Engine Refuses to Start from Cold/Engine won't Turn Over

Loose/corroded battery connections
Engine earth strap fixings loose
Battery flat – low electrolyte level
Starter connections loose
Solenoid faulty/loose connections
Starter jammed

Engine Turns Over but won't Fire

Fuel tank empty
Fuel pump faulty
HT lead connections poor
Coil connections poor
HT leads/distributor cap wet
HT leads faulty
Distributor cap cracked/arcing
Contact breaker points dirty/seized/gap incorrect
Spark plug end fittings loose
Spark plugs damaged/carbonned/oiled/wet
Spark plugs faulty/gap incorrect
Fuel pump defective/filter blocked
Engine flooded
Choke jammed on
Dirt in fuel bowl jet
Carburettor float seized

Start Motor Spins but Does Not Turn Engine

Inertia starter – low battery charge – broken drive spring
Inertia and pre-engaged starter motors – starter motor bolts loose
Pinion sticking

Engine Starts, but Runs Lumpily and Backfires when Revved

Spark plug/HT lead faulty

Engine wants to Fire but won't Run

Blocked air filters
Non-functioning choke
Air induction via vacuum pipe on inlet manifold
Faulty coil ballast resistor (later cars)

Engine 'Hunts'

Weak mixture from one carburettor

Engine Ticks Over Poorly on 3 Cylinders/ All 4 Fire When Revved

Breakage in copper-cored HT lead

ON-ROAD BREAKDOWNS

Engine Misfires or Loses Power

Fuel tank empty
Fuel filler cap breather blocked
Ignition components wet
Ignition open circuit
Faulty fuel pump
Blocked fuel filter
Sticking carburettor float

Engine Loses Power and Stops

Blocked fuel tank cap breather
Blocked fuel filter
Faulty fuel pump
Engine overheating

Engine Stops Without Warning

Ignition component failure

DEVELOPING PROBLEMS

Engine Overheats

Oil level low due to loss
Long-term problems – worn mains bearings – faulty oil pump – blocked oil pick-up strainer/filter – defective oil pressure relief valve

ENGINE OVERHEATS

Broken/slack fan belt
Faulty electrical cooling fan
Coolant leakage/internal blockage
Thermostat faulty
Engine oil level low
Brakes binding
Weak fuel mixture
Ignition timing fault

ENGINE BACKFIRES ON OVERRUN

Exhaust system leakage/burnt exhaust valve(s)

ENGINE SMELLS OF PETROL

A thankfully rare fault which can occur on Minis fitted with mechanical fuel pumps when the diaphragm is damaged. The earlier Type 700 can be stripped and a new diaphragm fitted; the later Type 800 is a sealed unit, and will have to be exchanged.

'GET-YOU-HOME' TIPS

The following .comprises advised courses of action which may enable you to effect temporary repairs; the advice must be used only in cases where it does not contravene prevailing national or local laws, and the author and publishers can assume no responsibility if advice does conflict with prevailing law.

In the UK., it is an offence to drive an 'unsafe' car on the public highway and, in fact, some police officers are being specially trained to detect any of 200 possible faults which render a car unsafe – they are empowered to prohibit the use of the car there and then. Serious problems which make a car unsafe to drive – including brake failure, lighting failure, almost any electrical, suspension or hydraulic problem – MUST be rectified before the car is driven.

Many developing faults give 'early warning' symptoms which the experienced driver can often recognise, giving you the chance to head straight for the nearest repair workshop or to stop the car before the fault develops further.

WHEN YOU ARE DRIVING THE CAR...

WATCH.
1. the engine coolant temperature gauge.
2. the oil pressure gauge.
3. the ignition warning light
IF.
1. temperature rises.
2. oil pressure falls.
3. ignition light comes on (commonly broken fan/generator drive belt).
THEN. Stop the engine as soon as is consistent with safety and investigate.

DEALING WITH ON-ROAD FAULTS

BROKEN FAN BELT. The 'fan' or more properly generator drive belt is driven by the crankshaft pulley and drives the water pump, engine cooling fan and dynamo on early cars, alternator on later cars. The usual first symptom of the broken belt is that the ignition light illuminates, signifying that the battery is no longer being charged.

A car with a broken belt can be driven gently for a very short distance but the lack of cooling effect from the fan, coupled with a lack of coolant circulation will quickly overheat the engine, and can result in internal engine damage. A battery in good condition will be able to power the ignition circuit for some time, although use of the lights, wiper motor, heater fan and especially the starter motor will reduce this greatly.

It is best to drive the car only to a known nearby place of safety or repair – don't drive away in the hope of finding something – the car could break down and leave you stranded in an even worse place.

Temporary fan belts are available, although those setting out on a long journey would do better to pack a spare belt, plus spanners and a lever with which to fit and tension it. The traditional 'get-you-home' ploy involves using a nylon stocking to make a temporary belt; variations include using leather belts and rope; the author has thankfully not had to resort to such botch-ups – pack a spare drive belt!

Broken Throttle Cable. Set the tickover to 1,500 rpm or slightly more, then change up through the gears to reach a top speed of circa 30 mph – and hope that you don't have to climb any steep hills!

Blowing Exhaust. Most of the sealing materials which the author has used offer strictly temporary repair – to make gums or bandage repair kits longer-lasting cover them with thin steel (from a drinks can, which can be cut with scissors) fastened with jubilee clips.

Broken Exhaust Mounting. These can usually be wired, but a jubilee clip repair will normally be longer-lasting.

Split Coolant Hose. Waterproof (self-amalgamating) tape will usually hold the few psi of the coolant, provided that the hose exterior is cleaned off first. Hoses with large splits will have to be replaced.

Binding Brakes. Allow to cool. The problem could be hydraulic or mechanical – unless you can find the reason for the binding and rectify it, progress should be limited to very short hops, stopping frequently and for long periods to allow the brakes to cool fully. Best to summon a recovery service.

Leaking Radiator. Proprietary repair substances are temporary measures only. Serious leaks need professional attention. Don't run the engine with no or low coolant.

Shattered Windscreen. Place cloth on scuttle and bonnet to catch glass, then use heavily gloved hand or implement to push ALL the shattered glass out. Open the windows and quarterlights to allow air to pass through cab.

DON'T

Hot wire the ignition – you'll have no indicators for one thing, and few of today's drivers recognise hand signals.

Drive with a flat tyre – it will soon come off the rim and damage both tyre and wheel – perhaps beyond repair.

Tolerate intermittent trifling electrical faults – some can suddenly become serious, permanent and terminal (both for the car and occupants).

Drive with seized brakes – fire hazard.

Live with any 'temporary' repair for a second longer than absolutely necessary.

Drive with an engine which is overheating or shows low oil pressure.

Replace a blown fuse with anything other than a fuse of the same rating – if this, too, blows, it is a warning of a short to earth which could directly cause an in-car fire.

NEVER

Drive with tyres under or over-inflated. This jeopardises roadholding, compromises handling and gives high tyre wear.

Use unleaded fuel unless the cylinder head had been specially modified.

TERMINAL FAULTS (SEND FOR THE CAVALRY)

These faults – thankfully – are all very rare, and most drivers will never suffer any of them. Should you be one of the unfortunate few, don't waste time – summon assistance at the earliest opportunity!

Mechanical Seizure. Engine – gearbox – differential.

Engine. Allow to cool fully. Don't use starter, but place in fourth gear and try to rock car backwards and forwards to see whether seizure has freed. Unless cause can be established and rectified (unlikely), don't run engine.

Fuel Pump Failure. Unless another pump can be fitted, summon assistance.

Appendices

FORECOURT DATA

Fuel

Cars to 1989	4 star leaded
Cars from 1990	optionally unleaded. (Ignition must be correctly set).

Lubricants and fluids

Engine/gearbox oil. Multigrade 20W/50, 10W/30 or 10W/40 engine oil. 10W/40 for all cars after 1983. Capacity 8.5 pints, 4.83 litres, 10.2 US pints. Automatic 9 pints, 5 litres.

Carburettor dashpot oil. As above.

Grease points. Lithium multi-purpose grease.

Brake and clutch hydraulic system. Hydraulic fluid to SAE J1703.

Anti freeze. To BS3151 or 3152. To -19 degrees C 33%. To -36 degrees C 50%.

Coolant capacity. 6.25 pints, 3.55 litres.

SERVICE DATA

Torque wrench settings

	Foot pounds	*Kg/metres*
Camshaft nut	65	8.9
Clutch spring set screws	16	2.2
Water temperature sender	16	2.2
Connecting rod big end nuts	33	4.6
bolts	37	5.1
Crankshaft pulley bolt	75	10.3
Flywheel driving strap set screw	16	2.2
Flywheel bolt	112	15.5
Flywheel housing nuts/bolts	18	2.5
Main bearing bolts	63	8.7
Manifold nuts	14	1.9
Oil filter centre bolt	14	1.9
Oil pump bolts	8	1.1
Oil pipe banjo	38	5.3
Oil relief valve nut	43	5.9
Cylinder head nuts	50	6.9
	Foot pounds	*Kg/metres*
Extra nuts 1275GT	25	3.5
Rocker cover	3.5	.5
Rocker shaft bracket nuts	24	3.2
Spark plugs	18	3.5
Oil sump drain plug	25	3.5
Timing cover/front plate bolts		
¼ in.	5	.7
5/16 in.	12	1.7
Cylinder side cover 1000cc	3.5	.5
Water pump bolts	16	2.2
Water outlet elbow nuts	8	1.1

Index